"Here Am I — Send Aaron!"

Jill Briscoe

While this book is designed for the reader's personal enjoyment and profit, it is also intended for group study. A leader's guide is available from your local bookstore or from the publisher.

VICTOR BOOKS

a division of SP Publications, Inc.

WHEATON. ILLINOIS 60187

Offices also in Fullerton, California • Whitby, Ontario, Canada • Amersham-on-the-Hill, Bucks, England

Seventh printing, 1981

Unless otherwise noted, Scripture quotations are from the King James
Version (KJV). Other quotations are from *The New Testament in
Modern English* (PH), © by J. B. Phillips, published by The Macmillan
Company; and *The Living Bible* (LB), Tyndale House Publishers,
Wheaton, Ill. All quotations used by permission.

Library of Congress Catalog Card Number: 77-93361
ISBN: 0-88207-767-8

VICTOR BOOKS
A division of SP Publications, Inc.
P.O. Box 1825 • Wheaton, Ill. 60187

To David, Judy, and Peter, who, when I got around to saying "Here am I, send me" let me go, with joy and love and precious willing hearts, to minister to other people's children. Thank you, kids. I love you.

Contents

Foreword

Some persons in the body of Christ are gifted for and committed to the vital task of preserving a highly technical science of interpretation of the Scriptures. We cannot forget the value of their contribution. However, in the stilted atmosphere of academia, the sheer excitement of learning and applying the glorious truths about life which God has invested in His Word is sometimes lost.

Jill Briscoe is an exciting person who is excited about God's truth revealed in His Book. She has given us in these pages a torch to kindle a sense of adventure and joy in the application of the Word to our lives. Many would find this believable had she chosen the New Testament for her format, but Jill has done a convincing job of contemporizing the Old Testament, bringing vibrancy and reality out of its pages. She whets our appetites for further exposure to this spiritual menu.

Many times I have been asked to suggest materials that would be helpful for group Bible studies. Jill's book will relieve the scarcity of such aids, since she not only teaches with her own captivating insight and wit, but throughout the book is challenging the reader to develop personal habits of Bible study. To assist us, she provides provocative questions and correlating passages at the end of each chapter. These would be profitable guides for either private or corporate study.

"Have you learned how to collect your manna, or is the Bible still a complete mystery to you? Are you frightened of it? Is it a big dark house that you are reluctant to enter?" Jill poses the questions, then addresses some resourceful answers, prodding her readers into the joyful adventure of reading, studying and applying the truth from God's Word.

Jill Briscoe has been fully captured by the Lord of the Book. He speaks to us through her. Thank you, Jill, for allowing Him to engage your talents and gifts to alert His body to the joyous responsibility of hearing Him and serving Him.

Elaine Stedman

1

The Big Dark House

"The Old Testament is like a big dark house, and I'm afraid to go inside," a teenager once said to me. Maybe that is how you feel about it. But if you dare to open the door, you will find the people who live there will welcome you in and switch on the lights, and you may see things you have never seen before. It's quite safe to visit for a while. In fact, you won't want to go "home" to the familiarity of the Gospel narratives, or even the well-worn epistles of the Apostle Paul. The honesty of the record, and the incidents with which you will identify will surely cause you to linger longer than you ever imagined possible.

Perhaps in the stories of Genesis we find an inability to identify. Building a huge portable zoo in the backyard is hardly a mid-America Saturday afternoon occupation, although we do have a couple of dogs and a canary! And then we might wonder what's so different about Jacob working for his wife for seven years when we've worked for ours for 20. A Bedouin tent and nomadic life-style may in some detail be reminiscent of IBM's fluid policy of moving its employees around, but all in all, the whole thing appears to have been lived out on another planet. It all seems to be a pocket of history that is totally unrelated to us.

I happen to believe, however, that the Book of Genesis is filled with relevant truth, the details of which can easily and adequately be applied to our modern-day situations. Leah, for example, knew what it was to have a husband who loved another woman, younger and more beautiful than she. I'm sure we can identify with the agony of Leah's rejection as we meet many of her sisters in our "family-collapsing" society. But I do understand that perhaps the parallels of the stories in the Book of Exodus hit nearer home for many of us than those in the Book of Genesis.

In 1 Corinthians 10:6-7, Paul stated, "Now these things were our examples, to the intent we should not lust after evil things, as they also lusted. Neither be ye idolaters, as were some of them; as it is written, 'The people sat down to eat and drink, and rose up to play.' " The stories of the Children of Israel in this Book were written for our example, that we should learn from their mistakes. It is to "these things" that we shall turn our attention.

Georg Hegel, a nineteenth-century philosopher, said, "What experience and history teach is this, that people and governments never have learned anything from history or acted on principles deduced from it." Let me humbly add a thought to the great man's words—people never have learned because they don't want to! But if they do want to, they can heed the example of these people, and be saved from similar failures in their Christian lives.

Would you be willing to learn lessons from history that could enrich and direct your life? Consider first of all Jacob's posterity:

Now these are the names of the children of Israel, who came into Egypt; every man and his household came with Jacob. Reuben, Simeon, Levi, and Judah, Issachar, Zebulun, and Benjamin, Dan, and Naphtali, Gad, and Asher. And all the souls that came out of the loins of Jacob were seventy souls; for Joseph was in Egypt already. And Joseph died, and all his brethren and all that generation. And the children of Israel were fruitful, and increased abundantly, and multiplied, and became exceeding mighty; and the land was filled with them (Ex. 1:1-7).

Jacob's religious heritage was rich with the promises of God concerning his children. Abraham and his descendants were possessors of promises which they carefully and meticulously passed on from generation to generation. The old patriarch was promised that the divine Son of God Himself would eventually come through his descendants. "And in thee shall all families of the earth be blessed" (Gen. 12:3). He would visit our disturbed planet (and its more disturbed inhabitants) to bring the peace of reconciliation through the sacrifice of Himself.

A Choice Vine

The nation of Israel, that is Abraham's sons, and sons' sons, was to be like a choice vine planted by Jehovah in a very fruitful hill, the Promised Land (Isa. 5:1). It would produce One whose life was pressed out on the cross of Calvary, and through whose shed blood the whole of mankind would celebrate.

In the Book of Exodus, we find the Divine Gardener transplanting His noble vine (Jer. 2:21) to His very fruitful hill. Halfway to fulfilling His Word, the vine rests in the land of Egypt, carried there through the providence of God, and nurtured for a time by Joseph. This man, you remember, had been miraculously led by the Divine Husbandman, and placed in the right position at the right time to preserve His chosen missionary nation. With this wonderful heritage of God's gracious choosing and blessing, we see the promises of God being worked out.

Having thought for a moment of Jacob's posterity and the privilege of Jacob's heritage, let us look at the prosperity of this man.

If you ask yourself, "How did Jacob become so prosperous in Goshen?" the answer is obviously because Joseph was there already! It was because of Joseph's position and influence that Jacob was blessed by prosperity in the land of

Goshen. Not only did the land of Goshen become a sanctuary from famine, but that pleasant land became a place for the vine to spread its boughs and run over the wall. That is exactly what the Scriptures say about the sojourn of the vine in Egypt: "Joseph is a fruitful bough, even a fruitful bough by a well, whose branches run over the wall" (Gen. 49:22).

But in the story of the vine transplantation, we sense an almost false sense of security among Jacob's descendants. The situation was deceiving. The writer of Exodus 1:6 wrote, "And Joseph died, and all his brethren, and all that generation." And in verse 8 he stated, "Now there arose up a new king over Egypt, which knew not Joseph."

The sons of Jacob found themselves living in the good of the blessings and influence of their past heritage. It was somewhat like a credit system. Just because their fathers had been blessed, they reckoned it would automatically continue. The Scriptures tell us a different story. The new king who came to power did not know Joseph, and didn't care for his sons. He brought the people who were born in Egypt into bondage. Their heritage didn't help them; they found the blessings of the past were no security for the present and the future. Having borrowed their parents' religion, it was now time for the sons of Jacob to pay their own way.

Let us pause for a moment and apply this to ourselves. Everybody starts in a place similar to Egypt. We are born into a world belonging to a prince that does not acknowledge Christ and is vehemently antagonistic to Him. Let us think of Pharaoh as representing Satan, who rules the nations of the world in which we live. Jesus acknowledged Satan's kingdom, and called him the "prince of this world" (John 14:30). Behind the Egyptian Pharaoh of our story in the Book of Exodus stands the "prince." The generation of Hebrews following Joseph were a people who were born in Egypt, slaves of Pharaoh, and in bitter bondage.

Until Pharaoh really began to make his presence felt, the people hardly realized their danger. The restraining influence of the past, and the privileges they had enjoyed for so long, prevented them from seeing the storm clouds gathering.

At the age of 18, living in England, I too considered myself secure in my religious heritage. Had not the fathers of my country believed in God, and built our land according to His principles? Great Christian men had liberated the oppressed and provided a haven of prosperity. I considered my nation "Christian" and was unaware I was trusting in a heritage, the results of which were almost past and gone. I thought myself a Christian simply because I was born in a Christian country.

It was not until I was old enough to feel the restraining chains of my slavery that I became aware that I was born in Egypt, and "Pharaoh" controlled my world and my life. The credit ran out—it was time to pay. Pharaoh doesn't really mind if we are dead or alive—as long as we are his. Sometimes he keeps us alive so he can use us to keep other people in bondage. He is a murderer at heart, but if he isn't murdering he is mastering, and worse, still using us to master others for him. Jesus tells us Satan was a murderer from the beginning (John 8:44). He cannot change—for a change presupposes something better or something worse. Since he is pure evil, he can't be worse; and as he will never be better, I'm afraid he remains the murderer he was from the beginning! Cain killed Abel, Haman sought to exterminate the Jews, the Pharisees were moved to crucify Christ, some Christians were burned at Nero's parties, and others were eaten alive by beasts. We have surely seen the murderer at work.

If Satan cannot murder, he will master. He doesn't really mind which. I suspect he prefers murder to mastering, for if we are alive, he knows there is always the chance we shall be delivered. However, he is under the control of the King who is greater than he is, and in whose hand our breath is, (Dan. 5:23), and when he has no option he will master us instead. Read Exodus 1:8-22:

> Now there arose a new king over Egypt, which knew not Joseph. And he said unto his people, "Behold, the people of the children of Israel are more and mightier than we. Come on, let us deal wisely with them; lest they multiply,

and it come to pass, that, when there falleth out any war, they join also unto our enemies, and fight against us, and so get them up out of the land." Therefore they did set over them taskmasters to afflict them with their burdens. And they built for Pharaoh treasure cities, Pithom and Raamses. But the more they afflicted them, the more they multiplied and grew. And they were grieved because of the children of Israel. And the Egyptians made the children of Israel to serve with rigor. And they made their lives bitter with hard bondage, in mortar, and in brick, and in all manner of service in the field; all their service, wherein they made them serve, was with rigor. And the king of Egypt spake to the Hebrew midwives, of which the name of the one was Shiphrah, and the name of the other Puah. And he said, "When ye do the office of a midwife to the Hebrew women, and see them upon the stools; if it be a son, then ye shall kill him; but if it be a daughter, then she shall live." But the midwives feared God, and did not as the king of Egypt commanded them, but saved the men children alive. And the king of Egypt called for the midwives, and said unto them, "Why have ye done this thing, and have saved the men children alive?" And the midwives said unto Pharaoh, "Because the Hebrew women are not as the Egyptian women; for they are lively, and are delivered ere the midwives come in unto them." Therefore God dealt well with the midwives; and the people multiplied, and waxed very mighty. And it came to pass, because the midwives feared God, that he made them [families]. And Pharaoh charged all his people, saying, "Every son that is born ye shall cast into the river, and every daughter ye shall save alive."

Maybe some of you who read these pages are thinking, "Well, it's all a bit dramatic. I don't feel I'm a slave of Satan. I really feel very free, and quite happy with myself and my life-style." Let me show you some characteristics of the one who is in bondage so you can recognize your position.

Tasks and Taskmasters

Pharaoh controlled the people by putting taskmasters over them. Satan has his taskmasters too. He uses tasks that master you, until you find yourself afflicted and burdened with things that you come to believe *have* to be done, or your world will fall apart. "Therefore they did set over them taskmasters to afflict them with their burdens. And they built for Pharaoh treasure cities, Pithom and Raamses" (Ex. 1:11). Think for a moment about the things you are busy doing. Have your tasks so mastered you that you have become burdened with them? The problem is, you have been kept so busy you haven't ever thought about it. Affliction may have come to your family simply because you have had to obey your taskmaster. Surely you are producing, you are even building cities! You are achieving visible results, but it's all for Pharaoh. The tasks that are busying you are not building a better relationship with your wife or husband and children, or making you more effective in your friends' lives.

It's just as if all that work and effort is producing a treasure city for other people to enjoy. You sweat it out, and they take all the credit and have the enjoyment of your labor. You have nothing to show at the end. Oh, you may have a brick or two now that Pharaoh allowed you to keep for wages, but in the end you will leave it all behind, for it is his. He is the prince of this world and everything here belongs to him. When a wealthy acquaintance died, I asked my husband about his will. "How much did he leave?" I asked. "Everything!" he replied. True, and as God asked in the Parable of the Rich Fool, "Then whose shall those things be?" (Luke 12:20) Are you building treasure cities for Pharaoh that will have to be left behind, or are you building something lasting in heaven?

A story is told of a wealthy man who labored with many tasks here on earth, and produced beautiful palaces in which he lived well and sumptuously, though selfishly, all his life. This man accepted Christ on his deathbed. He had a gardener who did not consider that his life consisted in the things he possessed (Luke 12:15). Delivered from the bondage of Egypt, his treasure was in heaven (Luke 12:33). Both died and went into eternity. The gardener was given a beautiful mansion. It had a marvelous view of the Sea of Glass, in full view of the Throne. The rich man was offered a hut— clean and white—but just a hut! Seeing his face fall, the Apostle Peter explained, "I'm sorry sir, but we did the best with the material you sent up!"

What are you busy building? Who are your taskmasters? What have you achieved of eternal worth? Let me tell you something; you will never build anything in heaven while you are in bondage in Egypt. You will come to the place where your tasks master you, and the whole thing becomes a bitter burden. Your taskmasters will drive you faster and faster until you are serving "with rigor." If only they would give you time to think, you would realize you were not created to be a slave of Pharaoh, but to be Jehovah's servant. A change of masters is imperative.

"And the Egyptians made the children of Israel to serve with rigor. And they made their lives bitter with hard bondage, in mortar, and in brick, and in all manner of service in the field" (Ex. 1:13-14).

There came a time in my own experience when I recognized that I was mastered, I had rationalized my sins and called it "growing up," simply because I would not admit to belonging to Pharaoh! My taskmasters kept me so busy I could take no time to think, but in the end, the burden was so great I came to the realization that I had done nothing of eternal worth up to that point in my life. Created to serve Jehovah, I served another master, even though I knew that God said, "Thou shalt have no other gods before Me" (Deut. 5:7). No one was better off because I had been around; no one was helped or blessed heaven for knowing me. True, I was friendly with some other slaves, but the only sharing we ever did was to rattle our chains in fellowship, or help each other build something else for Pharaoh. I discovered I needed delivering! Born in Egypt with a sinful nature—great religious heritage notwithstanding—I was a slave.

Read Exodus 2:23-25: "And it came to pass in process of time, that the king of Egypt died: and the children of Israel sighed by reason of the bondage, and they cried, and their cry came up unto God by reason of the bondage. And God heard their groaning, and God remembered His covenant with Abraham, with Isaac, and with Jacob. And God looked upon the children of Israel, and God had respect unto them."

In process of time, if we realize our position, and sigh and cry unto God by reason of our bondage, as the children of Jacob did—God will hear us and remember the promises He made to our forefathers. He will look, and He will see. He knows our plight, and has provided a way of escape. At the age of 18 I looked for and found the Provided Deliverer and was set free. Here is a prayer very like the one I prayed at that time which you can make your own, if you wish.

O God, You tell me I am born in sin; Satan has me where he wants me and I belong to him. I realize I'm captive to taskmasters that have kept me so busy, I haven't even had time to think about the things that really matter. But I've come to the point where I'm so pressured by it all, I've stopped long enough to feel the whip and acknowledge my need of deliverance. I need help! As You provided a deliverer for the Children of Israel, I read in Your Book that You have provided one for me. His name is Jesus and on Him I call right now. Hear me, Lord, save me from Pharaoh and from living a wasted life. Enter my life by Your Holy Spirit now, and set me free. Free to own another Master, whose service is perfect freedom.

Amen.

Worksheet for Group Study

Materials. Bible, notebook, and pencil. Suggested Bible translations to use in group—*King James Version,* or *New American Standard Version* (try to keep everyone with the same translation).

Time: One hour—any leftovers can be done as homework.

1. *Summarize by reading together Exodus 1:1-7.* Answer the following questions:

a. List the 11 names of the chief men of the households that came into Egypt with Jacob (vv. 1-4).

b. How many souls did Jacob beget? (v. 5)

c. Write a sentence in your own words describing the immediate history of the Children of Israel after Joseph's death (v. 7). Choose one or two members of the group to share their summary.

2. Look up these verses that speak of Israel as God's vine. Read them aloud to the group.

a. Genesis 49:22   Psalm 80:1-14
   Isaiah 5:1-2   Jeremiah 2:21

b. Discuss the question, *What did God expect of Israel?*

3. Discuss together the religious heritage of your country and name the things people rely on today, from their past Christian culture, that lull them into a false sense of spiritual security. Perhaps a word of testimony from the leader of the group can be given to this effect.

4. What does the Bible teach us about Satan influencing and controlling the affairs of our world?

a. Look up the following verses and write down a statement about them: Ephesians 6:11-12.
Share your findings with the group.

b. Read Daniel 10:10-14 and 11:1 in pairs.

   (1) What are these Scriptures saying about the evil spirits that stand behind the kings of our earth and influence their actions?

   (2) What do the verses teach us about God's good spirits, and their unseen activity? Share your finding with the group.

5. The taskmasters of today's world are many and varied. Serving them eventually leads to bitterness and a vexation of spirit. A list of them is to be found in the Book of Ecclesiastes, chapter 2.

This Book gives us a picture of a man with many taskmasters. The man's name is Solomon and even though he was king and supposedly free, he experienced the bondage of Pharaoh.

Name the masters he served that led him to the realization of his slavery.

Ecc. 2:1-2	Ecc. 2:7-8
Ecc. 2:3	Ecc. 2:9
Ecc. 2:4-6	Ecc. 2:10

If we obey these taskmasters we shall find ourselves building treasure cities for Pharaoh.

6. Read together Exodus 1:15-22. Discuss this statement: *What will it take for men and women to acknowledge their position and cry to God for deliverance?* Sometimes it takes the realization that to stay in Egypt will surely affect their children! Pharaoh hates children. He wants to destroy boys and bring girls into slavery. He uses the same taskmasters he uses for their parents. Sometimes it is a helpful incentive to unbelievers to point out to them that their children deserve more than a life in Egypt!

7. Prayertime.

a. Pause to enable any group members, who wish to do so for the first time, to ask God to deliver them from sin, Satan, and self. The leader may lead in a simple prayer.

b. Pray for people you know who are in bondage and don't or won't acknowledge it.

c. Pray for those who are relying on the faith of their fathers and have not yet exercised faith in Christ for themselves.

d. Pray for the children of people you know who are affected by a life lived in Egypt.

e. Ask God for a new revelation of the dreadfulness of a life in bondage in Egypt and a reminder of the bitterness you have been delivered from through Christ. Finish with praise for deliverance!

2

Delivered to
Be a Deliverer

The crocodiles must have been very frustrated. A nice meal of baby boy glided tantalizingly past them, but a protecting ark of bulrushes encased the child, and crocodiles don't eat bulrushes with their meat! Moses had never been safer, even though he was yelling fit to raise the mummies in the pyramids! He was on his way to the palace, though of course he didn't know it. God was looking ahead to the time when that vigorous baby boy returned to his people as His instrument of deliverance. But 80 years before that event something had yet to be done. Moses had to be delivered from judgment himself, before he could ever become a deliverer of others. Delivered to be a deliverer, that is Moses' story. The enveloping ark of bulrushes saved him from judgment, and though Pharaoh sought his life, he could not find him, for he was saved to serve. (Read Exodus 2:1-10.)

Here is our parallel. Judgment is pronounced on us. We who are born in Egypt are condemned already. Death is the sentence. The wages of sin is not suffering, as some think; the wages of sin is death (Rom. 6:23), and God has provided an ark. This "covering" beautifully typifies the work of our Lord Jesus on our behalf, in which we can rest, saved from destruction.

What are we saved for? Are we delivered simply to be slaves? No, a thousand times no! We are delivered to be deliverers. We are saved to serve. Many people ask Jesus Christ to forgive their sin, which He does, and they believe they are "in Christ" just as Moses was in the protecting ark of bulrushes. They believe they have been delivered from judgment, but they have no idea what they are supposed to be doing "now." Now is the time that God gives us, day after day, until "then." Then is the time when now finishes, and God asks us what we have been doing from "now till then!"

Do we understand that we are delivered to be deliverers? God has a work for each of us to do. Jesus was able to say, "I have finished the work which Thou gavest Me to do" (John 17:4). He was only 33 years old when He said that, and only three of those years had been spent in an itinerant ministry. But Jesus knew He was born at the right time, delivered from Herod to be a Deliverer. When the "then" came for Jesus, He was able to say "It is finished" (John 19:30). What was finished? The work of redemption God had given Him to do. If the then came for some of us at this moment, and God asked us about the work He had given us to do, many of us would have to say, "I haven't even started yet." One of the reasons for this sad state of affairs is that we do not know we have been delivered to be deliverers. There is a specific work assigned us. We are not saved by works, but we are saved "unto good works which God hath before ordained that we should walk in them" (Eph. 2:10). Part of these good works involves a "delivering" ministry.

Palace Training

So what did Moses do? Did he start trotting around as an evangelist at the age of four? No! He grew up first. God had to prepare His deliverer. He chose the best school of education He could find—the palace of Pharaoh. God has His marvelous ways of making training available to people who can't afford to pay for it through no fault of their own, or who are not "high born" enough to merit it! He simply arranged for the Princess to adopt His baby deliverer. Moses was to be prepared in the palace.

I want to say something here. Wherever God has allowed you to be brought up and educated, is His palace. Just because you may have had some bad experiences in your palace, as I'm sure Moses did, does not make it any the less His palace of preparation. There could have been no better training place for the work He has in mind for you! Pharaoh's palace would certainly not have been the choice of Moses' Hebrew parents, or perhaps of Moses himself, but God chooses to school us His way, knowing the work He has in mind for us in the future. Education and schooling must not be confused. The lessons learned in that heathen situation were to prove invaluable in the years ahead.

Think of the way God prepared His deliverer in his growing years. Moses would need to know how to read and write. After all, he was to be the author of a hefty part of a Book that was to be the world's best-seller! What better place to learn than in the royal school? He would need to understand the strategy of warfare, and in Pharaoh's palace he certainly would train for this. Government skills would be required as he ruled thousands of people; coordination, control, organization, and above all, the social graces and ability to tactfully inspire people would be necessary. What better training than the palace of the king? Pharaoh may have thought he was preparing Moses for the throne of Egypt, but God had another throne in mind. His own! One day in the "then" of eternity, Moses would cast his crown before his heavenly Deliverer and say to his Saviour, "I have finished the work You gave me to do."

We are not delivered to work for Pharaoh; we are delivered to work for God. But our preparation may well be in the palaces of a heathen king.

In the work God has given me to do in the United States, in the "now" of my life, I am constantly thankful for my palace preparation. My upper-class education enables me to understand and mix freely with people of like background. Sports involvement indulged in during my palace days, for sheer love of competition, has been used to contact people in this sports-crazy society. My drama training has been used constantly, and my teaching diploma has taught me how to break truth small enough for all to digest. I had no idea I was being prepared in the palace, but as soon as I was delivered to be a deliverer, at the age of 18, I began to put to use those skills acquired in His school.

We are not told just when Moses decided to be the deliverer he was delivered to be. God had surely chosen him, but there had to come a time when Moses had to choose for himself to do that chosen thing God had in mind. We don't know when, but we do know he did choose! Read Hebrews 11:24-29 and note the first word in verse 25. It is "choosing!" He chose to identify with the people of God. I have to wonder at the marvelous achievement of Moses' parents. "Take this child away, and nurse it for me, and I will give thee thy wages" the princess commanded the mother of the squalling baby (Ex. 2:9). The wages of Pharaoh's princess were nothing compared to the wages Moses' mother must have received, as she heard of her boy having come to years, refusing to be called the son of Pharaoh's daughter. Choosing rather to suffer affliction with the people of God, Moses was to grow to maturity with a very clear idea of which riches he desired, and they were *not* the treasures of Egypt. He chose freely the reproach of Christ, and the reward of heaven. What were the treasures of Egypt that Moses chose to do without? We are told that the treasures of Egypt, made available to Moses, would have brought him the pleasures of sin (Heb. 11:25). Note that sin can give you pleasure. Not joy, but pleasure, and that only for a season.

I had a marvelous time with good wholesome (and some not so wholesome) pleasure, before I chose the reproach of identifying with Christ and His people. But I came to realize something: the pleasure only lasted for a season. There began to be long gaps of time, in my experience, when I was simply waiting hopefully for some new pleasure to appear that might bring me lasting joy. But joy is something else. It does not depend on wealth, or position, or possessions, or any self-indulgence under the sun. Joy is Christ possessing you, and you possessing Him. And not for a season—but for always.

A Time in the Desert

Having chosen to identify with the people of God, Moses decided to become the deliverer he knew God had called him to be. Out of the palace he went to execute his first delivery. He hadn't gone very far before he found someone to save. Now he would begin the task God had entrusted to him. He saved his brother Jew, but lost his brother Egyptian (Ex. 2:11-12). What a start to his delivering ministry! Take heart if you have been discouraged by your first attempt to deliver someone. I'm sure you did better than Moses, and your efforts didn't end in murder. But you see, the preparation of the deliverer was not complete. Prepared in the palace he may have been, but something more was needed. A time in the desert! Moses needed a desert experience before he would ever be ready to deliver his nation. The problem with Moses was his temper. He simply could not control it. You will never liberate anyone else, if you have not experienced some measure of liberation yourself. In dangerous anger, Moses had carefully looked this way and that, and seeing no one, had committed homicide. His lack of self-control obviously had to be dealt with before he could ever be entrusted with the pastoral care of God's people. The Lord knew how many times in the future Moses would be stretched to the limit of his patience with the grumbling, mumbling Children of Israel, and if it took 40 years (which it did), God had to liberate him from that problem or there would surely be corpses stretched all the way into the Promised Land.

Moses was never completely liberated from his terrible temper, but he learned the self-control he needed to achieve God's goal for him. Remember how he came down from the mountain of God with the Ten Commandments in his hands, and how he found his people prostrating themselves in front of the golden calf? (Ex. 32:19) Do you remember what he did? That's right, he lost that old temper of his, and broke the Ten Commandments! (You always do, you know, when you lose your temper!) But progress had definitely been made—he did not break them over the people's heads, he broke them on the ground! Then he went back to God to start all over again; he had learned that in the desert.

It took God 40 years to prepare His deliverer to be a deliverer, so take heart. Don't go rushing out to save someone, as soon as you become a believer. Spend some time waiting on God for Him to show you His time and His way. If you have a gory testimony like Moses—hold it! Before you start delivering it, be prepared to grow up a little, so you are not speaking with great authority from the depths of your ignorance. Otherwise you will just end up hurting someone. John the Baptist was in the desert until the time for his showing to Israel (Luke 1:80). God told him when to start, and it was just the right moment.

You see, there's no avoiding the fact that it takes time to prepare a deliverer. It takes other things too. Crocodiles, bulrushes, palaces, and choosing to say "No" to the pleasures of sin. It takes failure, fear, flight, and forgiveness; and it will probably take a burning bush experience as well. Moses had to learn to deal with his memories, in the desert. He had to forgive himself for being the murderer God had already forgiven him for being. What God has forgiven and forgotten, we have no right to remember. God has said, "Their sins and their iniquities will I remember no more" (Heb. 8:12).

Moses had to learn to deal with monotony as well. I don't suppose there are many more monotonous tasks than 40 years of keeping sheep in the desert. Meditation is one antidote for monotony, and I'm sure Moses learned to stay his mind on a God who held the mysteries of heaven: the unraveling of which would sharpen his wits and inspire his thoughts, and so deal with the monotony of his occupation. Moses also married in his desert. I'm sure God realized he was going to need a little understanding of the ways and wiles of the fairer sex. And he would need to experience the problems of family life if he was ever to be counselor and friend to a city of families without a city. It's hard enough to help families when they have a home and a measure of security; but what to do when you march around in circles for 40 years with a million families at your back! Yes, Moses surely needed some personal experience in the matter of marriage. And so, in these three areas—memories, monotony and marriage—God prepared this man.

That's good news for you and me, isn't it? If I can take my palace education, and marry it to some desert experience, I have begun to grow. If I can learn to appreciate forgiveness, beat monotony with meditation, and use the lessons of my relationships at home to give me a greater sympathy and understanding of others, then I'm well on the way to being the deliverer I was delivered to be. You see, every born-again believer is obviously not a preacher or a teacher, but every true Christian is committed to Christ and realizes the need to be committed to others who are still in Egypt, and need to be saved. Not every Christian is a preacher, but every Christian is a witness.

A Very Ordinary Scrub Bush

Let us summarize Exodus 3:1-5. This very ordinary little scrub bush was simply sitting right under Moses' nose, minding its own business, when God decided to use it for a very special purpose. Maybe you can identify now. Perhaps you feel like a little scrub bush in a remote area of the desert. You are no different from 1,000 other little scrub bushes. You are quite insignificant and know you are not important at all—except, of course, to the little man or woman scrub bush who sits close to you in your desert world. But listen, little scrub bush, God needs you! You are growing just in the right place. What for? Well, God had a problem. His deliverer was mooching around with a lot of scraggy sheep for company in the desert. He was thoroughly defeated, discouraged, dry, disappointed, and possibly depressed. God's deliverer needed to be diverted so that the people could be converted. But how?

Well, God could use a little scrub bush to demonstrate His life . . . couldn't He? This way He could also show us that anything or anyone can be used as a vehicle of God. And that's just what He did. God had to somehow catch His man's eye. As the noted Keswick speaker, Major Ian Thomas, stated, "Any old bush will do!" In fact, God likes to use things and people that really are very ordinary, to let people see the extraordinary contrast of His presence within them. This way He gets all the glory, which is how it must be.

Let me add to Major Ian Thomas' statement by saying, "Any old bush can burn." The little scrub bush that diverted the deliverer's attention was demonstrating a truth to Moses that he needed to be reminded of. The truth was that the fire was God's! The writer of Hebrews 12:29 stated, "For our God is a consuming fire." And he stated in chapter one that He "maketh . . . His ministers a flame of fire" (Heb. 1:7). The dejected Christian who has run away from his work needs to be confronted by someone who hasn't, and is demonstrating a life in which the Holy Spirit burns with a consistency that demands investigation. How can a bush burn? Only by the operation of God. If a little scrub bush can be used, so can a forgiven murderer.

When Moses turned aside to see the little scrub bush, he found out that "any old bush would do" and "any old bush could burn," but he also found out that "any old bush could speak!" The Lord spoke from the heart of the bush! If I can never be a Moses, I can surely be a scrub bush, and allow Him to speak to others from the pulpit of my heart. One day, not many months later, the quiet of the desert was shattered, as thousands of people tramped past a very insignificant thorn bush on their way to Canaan. If the little scrub bush could have waved and prayed and rejoiced, it would have done so. In a very real way, God had used it to divert His deliverer, and send him on his way to do God's will. Back to Egypt he went to deliver his people from bondage into the glorious liberty of the children of God.

My mother-in-law, who is now resident in heaven, was used only once, as far as she knew, to lead someone to Christ. She had no way of knowing she was delivering a deliverer! That seven-year-old boy was just an ordinary little boy, and no one could know that 40 years later he would be used throughout the world to lead many, many people out of Egypt into Canaan. As I have had the privilege and joy of watching that particular bush burn for over twenty years, I know one person is not more important than the other. Each to his task, that's all. Stuart Briscoe or Mary Briscoe did not compete for a reward based on the numerical results of their ministry. One bush may have a greater capacity to reveal Christ than another, but we are all nothing without Him, and "any old bush can burn!" The incredible thing to me is that God uses the "foolish things of the world to confound the wise . . . the weak things of the world to confound the things which are mighty, and base . . . and . . . despised [things] . . . which are not, to bring to [nothing] things that are" (1 Cor. 1:27-28). It seems incredible until I read 1 Corinthians 1:29 and find the reason: "That no flesh should glory in His presence."

So whoever you are, a Moses or a scrub bush, will you burn for Him? A deliverer must be diverted so the people may be converted! Your time may have arrived; perhaps your preparation is complete and it's time to take off your shoes. That means you need to be very careful how and where you walk from now on—for the place where you stand, when you finally face up to your call and your responsibilities, is holy ground.

Maybe some who read these words would like to burn, but are afraid. It all sounds rather uncomfortable—all that fire and smoke and flames! Perhaps there are some little crooked parts of your scrub bush you like too well, and you don't want them to be destroyed. If you let God set you alight with His presence, what will be left of you? Notice what the Bible says about the scrub bush: "the bush burned with fire, and the bush was not consumed" (Ex. 3:2). How invigorating is the fire of God that He imparts to those who choose to choose what He has chosen for their life!

So turn aside to see, won't you?

Worksheet for Group Study

Each of these sections deserves close attention and much discussion. I suggest the class be split up into six groups. The groups should not be larger than six or eight people. If there are more in the class, divide into 12 groups, and ask each group to start and study a different section.

Group 1.   Numbers 1—2
Group 2.   Numbers 3
Group 3.   Numbers 4
Group 4.   Numbers 5
Group 5.   Numbers 6
Group 6.   Numbers 7—8
Group 7.   Numbers 1—2
Group 8.   Numbers 3
Group 9.   Numbers 4
Group 10.   Numbers 5
Group 11.   Numbers 6
Group 12.   Numbers 7—8

When the groups have finished, they can take any of the questions and try and finish the worksheet. At the end of the hour, allow 15 minutes for the class leader to receive a short summary of each question from the groups. This way a sketch of all the points will be received.

The prayertime can be conducted after the summaries have been shared.

1. Read Exodus 2:1-10 round the group.
Identify (as I have suggested in chapter 2) what each of the following things or people can represent.

    a. The crocodiles on the Nile
    b. The ark of bulrushes
    c. Moses
    d. Pharaoh

2. Turn to John 17:1-3 and read it to yourself.

    a. Share with the group what you think Jesus had finished.

    b. Why is it important for us to discover the work God wants us to do?

    c. Can anyone suggest one thing God expects all of us to include in our agenda, in our "now till then"?

3. I want you to think for a minute or two about your palace upbringing. Each one in the group will be different. Go round the circle, trying to share one thing in your background that has contributed to making you unique. Can you think of one thing you are thankful for which you can see could be part of God's preparation for your ministry?

4. Define in your notebook the difference between the pleasures of sin and the joy that identification with Christ brings.

5. Look up the following verses about real joy. Memorize one this week that is especially meaningful to you.

Nehemiah 8:10	Matthew 13:20
Psalm 16:11	John 15:11
Psalm 30:5	Acts 20:24
Psalm 51:12	Hebrews 12:2
Psalm 126:5	James 1:2
Isaiah 12:3	Jude 24

6. If we will not choose to go to a desert place apart with God, He will lead us or drive us there.

    a. Discuss the reasons people will not spend time with God to grow up.

    b. Share some personal hard lessons learned about service without preparation.

    c. Look up the following verses concerning the desert habits of our Lord Jesus. Read them out round the group: Matthew 26:36; Matthew 4:1; Matthew 14:23; Luke 6:12.

    7. God not only shapes us for His service in the palace, but also in the desert, with some very ordinary tools. Do you remember just three of these I suggested to you? God not only used these shaping circumstances in Moses' life, but I suspect He uses them in ours also. They were: memories, monotony, and marriage.

    Anyone can:

    a. Share with the group how any of these have *prevented you* from being a deliverer and why.

    b. Share how experiences within any of these areas have contributed to making you a *better deliverer*.

    8. Discuss the following statement: "I have to have complete victory over bad habits in my life before I can witness to the people in Egypt." (Remember Moses.)

    9. Turn to 1 Corinthians 1:26-31.

    a. Make a list of the qualifications of the man or woman, boy or girl, that God has called.

    b. Why does He choose such scrub bushes? (v. 26)

    10. Summary time with leader.

    11. Pray "in" all you have been talking "out" in your group. Keep your prayers short, to the point, and honest.

3

Here Am I, Lord, Send Aaron

God had to find a way for His deliverer to be diverted so the people could be converted. He used the little scrub bush to catch His man's attention, but not until Moses turned aside to see did the Lord call to him from the midst of the bush. Read Exodus 3:1-4.

We have to do certain things if the call of God is to be confirmed in us. We have to take the time to turn aside and investigate a quality of life that has perhaps arrested us in another person. We have to seek out the man or woman of God we have passed by day after day, and turn aside to see, to ask, and to humbly inquire after their precious secret. We have to want to know the secret of the burning heart.

When Moses turned aside to see, he discovered that secret. The secret of the burning heart is simply the centrality of the Lord. "God called unto him out of the midst of the bush" (Ex. 3:4). If the Lord is not central, there will be no fire, there will be no difference at all. The lordship of Christ in our lives simply means He is the One around whom everything else in our lives revolves. All too often we are the centers of our lives and everyone else, including the Lord Jesus, is expected to revolve around us. Lordship means He is the Lord of the ship.

When the Lord saw that Moses turned aside to see, He called out. What did He say? "Moses, Moses!" Well, that was quite something. He could have said, "Hey, you dirty, rotten murderer," or He could have said, "Hey, you lousy, lazy good-for-nothing, time-wasting sheepherder." He didn't. He said, "Moses, Moses!" Moses, we are told, means "to draw out." Do you remember that in Exodus 2:10, Pharaoh's daughter named him Moses when she drew him out of the Nile? Perhaps God used His own special name to remind this man that He loved him and had come to draw him out of defeat and lead him into victory. To draw him out of oblivion and disillusionment and make him a name in the earth and a blessing to a nation. God's will is ever to draw us out of our backwater, wherever it is, and when we are ready to turn aside and see, speak to us in love and mercy.

Suddenly, Moses was aware of something. His shoes! You don't stand in front of God with your shoes on; you take them off. Try it sometime; walk into your bedroom and stand, as it were, in His Presence. Then bend down and take off your shoes. How do you feel? I suppose in our day and age, we would take our hats off if we were men, or cover our heads if we were women. I don't know, but I do know when you take your shoes off, it makes you feel kind of silly, and small, and just about the size we really are before God. It's holy ground, you see, and it's holy because He's standing on it too. The One who has feet like burnished brass places them alongside your little crooked ones. When I think of His feet, that span the worlds—as He steps with easy tred from universe to universe, leaving the unmistakable imprint of His size on the face of the planets—and then think of my little feet standing in the same place, I am overwhelmed, and I whisper as Moses did, "Here am I." We feel so overawed by it all. The sudden heat from the fire of His Presence is too much and we somehow feel it necessary to tell Him we are here. So small we are, so small we feel; we are sure He cannot see us, even though He has called our name!

But listen, He says something else. "I am the God of thy

father, the God of Abraham, the God of Isaac, and the God of Jacob" (Ex. 3:6). "Moses, I am the God of your family," He said, and being a God who cared carefully for His own, He was about to do something about the lost members.

A Holy Fear

Moses hid his face! There he stood with his shoes off in front of a bush that blazed, on ground that trembled with the weight of God's glory, and he couldn't look, for he was afraid. Moses knew what it was to be afraid. He had been afraid before. In Exodus 2:14, we read that Moses was afraid when he realized somebody knew about the murder he had committed. He was afraid of Pharaoh; that's why he had run away, and now he was afraid of God! That's good. Until we are more afraid of God than we are of Pharaoh, we will never become a deliverer.

When we turn aside to see, and hear Him call our name and feel the impact of His being, then we will be afraid. Oh, holy fear! Then we shall be wise and know easily what is the work He has given us to do, for "the fear of the Lord is the beginning of wisdom" (Prov. 9:10). We shall never have any trouble discovering His will for our lives if we are frightened enough of Him to make sure we find out.

I can hear some of you saying, "Whoa! Wait a minute. I'm not frightened of God; He's my Friend." Moses was frightened of God—he saw His face and he was frightened. He heard His voice and he was afraid. He stood as near to the full power and presence of God as any of us and he hid his face. He didn't say there's nothing to be frightened of. There was. He was facing a God of red hot abilities!

I want to tell you, when I have drawn aside to really see God, and He has spoken to me, I have been left with a sense of the awfulness of God that devastates me. I take off my shoes, cover my face, and I cry, "Here am I, but who are You? You are so bright and light and right and mighty; be careful of me, God, or I am lost." My humanity trembles before His divinity. It must, it will, it is right that it should.

Like Job, I have to say, "I have heard of Thee by the hearing of the ear: but now mine eye seeth Thee. Wherefore I abhor myself and repent in dust and ashes" (Job 42:5-6).

Yes, He is my Friend, but He is my fiercely holy Friend, and I am "afraid." Only as I rightly fear Him will I cease to fear Pharaoh and be ready for my orders.

The Four Ds

I made a statement that we shall easily know the work God has given us to do if He is in the center of our lives. If we take time to turn aside to see Him, we will see Him in the Scriptures, and hear Him speak to us.

Look at Moses. Do we see him casting about in his mind wondering what it was God wanted him to accomplish? Of course not. It was clearly and carefully spelled out to him (Ex. 3:6-10). There was no doubt whatsoever left in Moses' mind about the nature of the work God had given Him to do. Nor will there be in yours, my friend.

In fact, if you want me to give you a clue to what it is, I will! First of all, it will be a delivering work: "And I am come down to deliver them out of the hand of the Egyptians, and to bring them up out of that land unto a good land and a large, unto a land flowing with milk and honey; unto the place of the Canaanites, and the Hittites, and the Amorites, and the Perizzites, and the Hivites and the Jebusites" (Ex. 3:8). Secondly, it will be a dangerous work (you don't take on Pharaoh and escape unscathed): "Come now therefore, and I will send thee unto Pharaoh, that thou mayest bring forth my people, the children of Israel, out of Egypt" (Ex. 3:10).

Thirdly, it will be a disappointing work: "And the Lord said unto Moses, 'When thou goest to return into Egypt, see that thou do all those wonders before Pharaoh, which I have put in thine hand: but I will harden his heart, that he shall not let the people go' " (Ex. 4:21). Anyone engaged in the delivering ministry knows you have to have an infinite capacity for being let down. Fourthly, it will be a directed work!

"And I am come down to deliver them out of the hand of the Egyptians" (Ex. 3:8). So my friend, I have no idea where the people are that are yours to deliver. I don't know where they live or how they live, but I know they live in a place within your reach, and I know God would draw you out and call you "Moses," pointing out to you the exact ones He wants you to deliver. And I know as surely as you have been delivered to be a deliverer, as every child of God is called to be, you will need to face Pharaoh on their behalf, fearing the danger of your Lord's displeasure rather than the wrath of him who holds your people in his power. I know surely there will be tremendous disappointments ahead for you, but I know also that disappointments are His appointments. These things I can tell you.

"Come now," said God to Moses, "and I will send thee unto Pharaoh!" Why? "That thou mayest bring forth My people out of Egypt."

The Exercise of Prayer

One of the first things you need to learn in the deliverance ministry is the exercise of prayer. You see, the people God wants you to deliver are bondslaves to Pharaoh. Satan has them in chains. Overseen by his taskmasters, they are too busy to lay down their tools and listen to you. In fact, if they do, Satan will make it hard for them. Read Exodus 5:10-23.

But pray on, because the fantastic thing is that no matter how weak a Christian you are, God wants you to challenge Pharaoh, and say to him in the name of the Lord, "Let my people go!" Now note, you have to stand in front of Pharaoh in the name of the Lord. God was careful to instruct Moses about that (see Ex. 4:21; 5:1). We dare not face the prince of this world without the authority of the King, but in His name we dare, and we must. Someone has said, "The devil trembles when he sees the weakest saint upon his knees."

What is in this name? God said to Moses, "I am the God of thy father, the God of Abraham, the God of Isaac, and the God of Jacob." Moses' ancestors had known God by the name,

Elohim, which means Almighty, Strength, All-Powerful Creator. Satan is powerful, but always remember that Satan is a created being and as such, lesser than the One who created him. That is why to come in this name was to present Pharaoh with the authority of the One who permitted his evil existence for His good pleasure.

And so, the first step in delivering someone is to start praying for them, believing each time you stand and demand their release from Pharaoh, that one of their chains drops to the ground.

The second step in delivering someone is to stop talking with God about it and get up and do something. "What?" you ask. Go and talk to them! Immediately, I hear some of you raising all sorts and sizes of arguments. If you are objecting, you find yourself in good company, for that is just what Moses did.

The first thing Moses said, in response to the call of God, was, "Here am I." Then when the orders were spelled out he started to argue. "Here am I, but who am I?" he asked. "I'm too little and the job's too big!" God agreed he was little, but reminded him that He wasn't. He was twice the size of Pharaoh and then some. "Certainly *I* will be with thee," He reminded Moses. And so the little "i" could hold hands with the big *I*. They would go together. That question answered, Moses tried another one. "Here am I, but who are You? I don't know enough about You—why, I don't even know Your name, and if I don't even know Your name, how ever am I expected to introduce You to others?"

God answered this one by simply explaining Himself to Moses. He told him His name—one that neither Moses or any other person had ever heard until that very moment. He then explained the name meant that He was fully committed to being involved in the buying back of His people from Pharaoh's grip and ownership. In fact, He explained that His name *I AM* meant "I will be all that is necessary as the occasion arises."

God didn't ask Moses to go and explain all he didn't

know about God; He just asked him to go and explain all he did know! It wasn't very much—he had just learned His name—but apparently God expects us to go and tell others the little we do know, and not worry about the lot we don't. The little we do know will be enough if God directs us to tell it.

And Moses Went

Moses then tried, "Here am I, but they won't listen." Let us read God's answer to that one, in Exodus 4:1-9. "If they won't listen," said God, "show them a miracle!" That'll do it. Now there are a few miracles recorded in verses 1-9. There is the miracle of a rod becoming an angry snake that caused Moses to run. There is the miracle of Moses' hand becoming leprous when he put it inside his cloak, but I would like to respectfully point out the biggest miracle. You will find it in Exodus 4:29. "And Moses . . . WENT." *That* was the biggest miracle. When Moses came out of his desert of defeat a changed man—obedient, chastened, courageous (remember he was wanted for murder), and went back to the people who had rejected him and a king who hated him, the Children of Israel witnessed a miracle.

I don't intend to get into the subject of miracles here, but just let me say that God is able to do anything He wants to do. Anything He has done in the past, or present, and everything He has never done yet in the past or present or will do in the future, He is able to do. A miracle is simply God being Himself, adapting His laws or changing them. But the greatest miracles I have seen on earth are those concerned with changed lives. It's comparatively simple, though still miraculous, for God to operate His power on an inanimate stick, but to take Moses the killer and turn him into a saver of lives is miracle indeed. When the Children of Israel see that, they will believe!

"Here am I, but who am I?" "Here I am, but who are You?" "Here I am, but they won't listen!" All were answered. But still the arguments came. Finally the most familiar of all suggestions came forth from Moses. It's that same familiar argument that God's called and chosen deliverers still present today. You will find Moses' last objection in Exodus 4:10-18. What was it? "Here I am, Lord, send Aaron!"

Oh, how God must get sick and tired of hearing that! "I'm slow of speech, and of a slow tongue!" (v. 10) As my husband once said, "That was a funny thing to say, because he was pretty quick with the excuse!"

God answers us as He answered Moses. "I made your mouth" (v. 11). "I know how fast your tongue can wag, and really, the speed doesn't matter, it's the message that it brings. You will find, if only you will be obedient, that it shall be given you in that hour what you shall speak!"

When the time comes for you to leave your palace or desert days and obey the call of God, don't say, "Here am I, Lord, send Aaron." It's a wasted argument because God may answer that request fully, but He also intends to send you right along with Aaron. God is committed to the people in bondage, and even though He may have to become angry with us (v. 14), He is determined to send us on our way. Maybe He will even send a "brother" into our desert to accompany us and show us how to carry out His orders (vv. 27-28).

I remember the first time I ever went to speak to a soul in "Egypt." God gave me an "Aaron" who could speak better than I. She was older and more courageous than I. We went together to speak to a girl, and then another and another on our college campus. It didn't take long for me to interrupt her presentation and take over. God knew what He was doing. When you can't go by yourself, take someone with you: an Aaron. But whatever you do, don't tell God to send him and not you. He won't listen.

It's interesting to note that in Exodus 5:1, the writer stated that Moses and Aaron told Pharaoh, "Thus saith the Lord. . . ." In Exodus 5:3 it's still "they said." In chapter 7:1-2, Aaron is still doing the speaking, but we arrive at chapter 8:9-10, and read that *"Moses* said unto Pharaoh."

Look at Exodus 12:21—from then on it's Moses all the way.

Will you turn aside, as Moses did, to see? Will you take off your shoes, will you be afraid of God (in the right sense), will you go to Pharaoh and tell him to let God's people go? Or will you argue and say, "Here am I, Lord, send Aaron"? He won't listen, for the time has come. He may send you an Aaron to support and encourage you as you start, but in time He will expect you to be saying, "Thus saith the Lord!" All on your own!

Worksheet for Group Study

1. Look up the following accounts of men who took time out to turn aside and see a special manifestation of God. Isaiah 6:1-8; Daniel 7:9-10; Revelation 1:10-16; Jeremiah 1:1-10; Job 42:5-6

    a. What did they see of special significance concerning the character of God?

    b. What was their immediate reaction?

    c. What was their final response or long-term commitment?

2. Why should we fear God? Is He not our Friend? Is He perhaps our "fearful Friend"? Look up the following verses: Psalm 19:9   Mark 4:40   Proverbs 1:7

3. The work God has called every believer to do may have the following aspects:

A Delivering Work. 2 Corinthians 4:1-7

A Dangerous Work. John 15:18-20; Matthew 10:16-28

A Disappointing Work. Ezekiel 3:1-11; Amos 7:10-13 Luke 9:44-45; 2 Corinthians 4:8-11; John 14:1-9.

A Directed Work. John 14:15-18; Matthew 28:19-20. Discuss or meditate on your findings.

4. Read Luke 11:1-13. Discuss the following:

    a. Is not "importunity" counted as vain repetition or lack of faith?

b. Read Ephesians 6:12. Does this verse give us a clue to the reasons for importunity in prayer?

5. Discuss, or write down on a piece of paper, the excuses you have for not being involved in a delivering ministry. Compare Acts 7:22 with Exodus 4:10.

6. Pray about these things. Can you say "Here am I, Lord, send me"?

4

Between the Devil and the Deep Red Sea

We come now to the contest with Pharaoh (Ex. 5:1-2). "Let My people go," demanded God through the lips of Moses and Aaron. "Why should I?" demanded Pharaoh, behind whose physical being stood the enemy of men's souls.

At once the situation worsened for the Children of Israel. Pharaoh tightened his grip upon them. This can almost be a good sign for us when we are praying for loved ones, for as we come in prayer, in the name of Jehovah God, seeking to demand of Pharaoh that he release the slaves he has in bondage, we can expect him to do just what Pharaoh did, and tighten his grip.

I remember the Reverend Dick Rees speaking about how he witnessed to his brother, Tom. Tom became violently antagonistic toward the Gospel message, and toward his brother, the Gospel's messenger. In fact, the more believing prayer was made on his behalf, the worse his attitude became. He wouldn't listen to Dick, and he became even more busy, burdened, and bitter, just like the Children of Israel (Ex. 6:9). This apparent hardening of attitude tells us something. Satan is worried. So pray on, and believe that soon they will be free. We must believe God for their deliverance. We must believe for those who cannot believe for themselves.

Pharaoh wouldn't listen, and neither would the Children of Israel. So God decided to add another voice to the argument: the voice of the plagues.

"Let my people go to let my people grow," demanded Moses. That's the only way they will ever serve Jehovah. "Let My people go, that they may serve Me," God demanded through His mouthpiece (Ex. 8:1). "No man can serve two masters" (Matt. 6:24). We have been told that we should serve God only (Matt. 4:10). The problem with many people today is that they think they can serve God in Egypt. They think going to church or saying prayers, reading the Bible or just believing in God, is serving Him. But the service God required was in Canaan, in a different dimension altogether. They were to be free from Pharaoh's jurisdiction, and released to offer acceptable sacrifices (Ex. 3:18).

But Pharaoh hardened his heart, and that is always a very dangerous thing to do. If you harden your heart long enough, and often enough, God will harden it for you in the end. He will give it a fixed setting (Ex. 11:10).

God began to make natural phenomena behave in an unusual way. It is one of God's methods to use the miracle of the ordinary to speak of Himself to mankind. For example, in Romans 1:20, Paul wrote, "Since earliest times men have seen the earth and sky and all God made, and have known of His existence and great eternal power. So they will have no excuse when they stand before God at Judgment Day" (LB).

But if we won't pay attention to the still small voice of creation, that insists silently that God is worth listening to, then He has to use a megaphone. This He did in the Book of Exodus. He used polluted water, famine, corrupted crops, ecology, sickness, and death.

Still Pharaoh hardened his heart. The same situation exists today. People are like Pharaoh, and do not always respond to God because of their adverse circumstances.

The plagues that God allows to come into their lives can be either plagues of deliverance or plagues of defiance. People react in totally opposite ways. We read in Revelation 16:9, "And men were scorched with great heat, and blasphemed the name of God, which hath power over these plagues; and they repented not to give Him glory." In Revelation 16:11, the writer states that the people suffering from the God-permitted plague "blasphemed the God of heaven because of their pains and sores." To these people, the plagues that God allowed to touch their lives brought a reaction of defiance. Actually, Pharaoh acted like many of us do. While the plague was plaguing him, he softened, but when respite came, he hardened his heart. That sort of behavior isn't too different from mine or from that of some believers I know.

It wasn't that Pharaoh and his servants weren't convinced God was speaking to them: "This is the finger of God" his magicians exclaimed after Moses' rod had swallowed up theirs (Ex. 7:19). Everyone recognized the power of Satan, but even the unbelievers recognized the power of God that was greater. Yet they continued to defy Him.

Pharaoh's Proposals

The people who really wanted to believe in God's promises, on the other hand, began to hear the voice of God in the awful happenings around them. Those who were about to be delivered began to dare to look up, for their redemption was drawing nigh. They were ready. They recognized Moses as their spokesman, and they experienced the results of his prevailing prayer on their behalf. They felt the tyrannical grip of Pharaoh loosen, but then Pharaoh began to bargain, as Pharaoh always will when his hand is forced.

The proposals that Pharaoh offered to the Children of Israel are the same Satan offers people today. Satan had to think up a proposal that would make his slaves decide to stay in Egypt, of their own free will. The first one we have already touched on. You can read about it in Exodus 8:25. "Live in Egypt, serve me, and sacrifice to God in your bondage." What Pharaoh was suggesting was "a form of godliness, but denying the power thereof" (2 Tim. 3:5).

I was once asked to have a young girl to stay in our home. She was only fifteen, and her parents were nearly demented because she was seeing a twice-married man, who still was married. His wife was not aware of the situation, but the girl's parents had discovered the relationship and wanted to get her away from the temptation for a period. The parents of the girl, however, were not Christians, and did not want their daughter to leave Egypt either. They just wanted her set free from that particular taskmaster. "Please have her to stay with you, Jill," they implored, "but don't convert her or anything like that! We just want her to have enough religion to make her respectable." Sacrifice in bondage! It's a proposal of Pharaoh, for he knows that "if the Son therefore shall make you free, ye shall be free indeed" (John 8:36). That means coming out of Egypt altogether, into a totally new experience.

Having failed to get Moses to comply with his request, Pharaoh put forward his second proposal. "Stay in sight. Don't get too involved. You don't have to go very far away. Why not leave an escape route so you can come back and serve me if you don't like it out there?" (Ex. 8:28)

A little boy fell out of bed one night. When his mother asked him what had happened, he said, "I guess I stayed too near where I got in!" Exactly! Many people are tempted by Pharaoh to do just that—stay too near where they got in. "Leave your options open," Satan says, "stay in sight." But this will never work, for you can't even see Canaan from Egypt. Moses answered this as he had the previous proposals, "Thus saith the Lord God of the Hebrews, 'Let my people go.'"

The next suggested compromise is recorded in Exodus 10:8-11. "You that are men, go—but leave your families behind. Don't involve everyone. Please don't think of encouraging others to go. If you have to go, then go, but don't take your loved ones with you."

When people are on the verge of being delivered, one of Satan's suggestions is often to imply that the whole business could well cause real division in the family. "Maybe some of your loved ones won't want to go with you into your promised land. Then what will you do?" Satan may ask. "There may even be trouble, and you've troubles enough already. It's not fair to get into this without your family, and it's too hazardous to take them into the wilderness with you." In this way, he uses what may happen to prevent you from being delivered.

Moses simply replied that it was God's will that *all* the family have the opportunity to go, and it was the Father's responsibility to see that they had the chance.

Pharaoh had nearly finished fighting with words. With lice, mice, locusts, and frogs coming out of his ears, he made one desperate suggestion.

"All right, go if you must, but leave your cattle and goods behind you," he said (Ex. 10:24).

But the cattle would be needed, and so would the goods. All we have and are is needed to serve our God. "Not a hoof must be left behind," Moses insisted (Ex. 10:26). Sacrificing to Jehovah involves everything. A Christian commitment is not merely a spiritual thing, but a life-style touching the warp and woof of everyday life. Our person *and* our possessions are all involved.

The Passover

The contest was nearly over. The proposals of Pharaoh had been rejected. It was time to be delivered. What was it going to take to make Pharaoh finally release the Children of Israel? It would take the death of the firstborn! And just as it would take the death of Pharaoh's firstborn to force him to set the people free, so, thousands of years later, the firstborn of God, Jesus Christ, would set the world of slaves free! Now obviously Pharaoh did not want to let them go, but Jesus, in stark contrast, came to set men free. The death of Christ was prefigured in the lamb that would play its vital part in the people's redemption.

The death of the lamb, a picture of the beloved Son of God, would forever be part of Israel's heritage.

God is a God of justice, but God is also a God of love. In love God warns, and in love God commands. Love that lays no limits isn't love. And love's limits have been outraged by sinful man's trespasses, so that God must judge. Even though God must judge, He also must love.

The dilemma of a just God who is love was solved for sinful man when He told the people in bondage, "Take a lamb." The pattern was set. The Children who would be delivered were to take a lamb without blemish and without spot (Ex. 12:1-11).

These people had no way of knowing the eternal significance of the instructions they were given. But as they obeyed and kept the Passover in succeeding generations, this action picture of our Redemption spoke louder than words could ever have done.

The lamb, without blemish and without spot, spoke of the Lord Jesus, "the Lamb of God which taketh away the sin of the world" (John 1:29). The little lamb, kept four long days under scrutiny to validate its perfection, proved to the Children of Israel its innocence and therefore its qualifications. The Lord Jesus, kept under the hostile scrutiny of His enemies, was able to enquire of them, "Which of you convicteth Me of sin?" (John 8:46) None could accuse Him, for the Lamb was indeed without blemish and without spot.

The lamb of the Exodus had to be one year old. The age of innocence with the nature of meekness, beautifully prefiguring The Lamb who was to be "brought to the slaughter and as a sheep before her shearers is dumb, so he openeth not his mouth" (Isa. 53:7).

The lamb of the Exodus had to be killed in the evening at the ninth hour, and if you remember, we are told in Matthew 27:46, "And about the ninth hour Jesus cried with a loud voice . . . 'My God, My God, why hast Thou forsaken Me?'" Having killed the lamb at the ninth hour, the people in Egypt then had to apply the blood to the door lintel of their home. In Leviticus we are told that life is in the blood, and in Hebrews 9:22 it is stated that "without shedding of blood is no remission [of sin]." By a life given, there was to be deliverance from judgment.

Christ, our Passover, was sacrificed for us 2,000 years ago (1 Cor. 5:7), and if we personally apply that lifeblood poured out for our sins, the God of justice will pass over us! (Ex. 12:13) Jesus Christ was the Lamb slain for you personally from the foundation of the world (Rev. 13:8).

And so the time arrived. Death came in judgment to every home without the blood of a passover lamb upon its doorposts. Cries of agony ascended into the darkened skies, and Pharaoh finally let the people go. It took the death of his firstborn for him to loosen his evil grip, just as it would take the death of God's firstborn to loosen Satan's grip forever on the souls of men.

Redemption

The people were ready. They had been told to eat the passover meal in haste, ready for flight, and when the time came, we read that they went out in one big dash. They just took off, glad to be free, thrilled to be rid of Pharaoh's land and his taskmasters' whips. Their excitement and joy knew no bounds. They were gripped by a sort of euphoria. The visible Presence of God was right there with them. Day and night His Presence could be seen manifested in either a cloud or a pillar of fire. What a fantastic experience that was. Everyone was involved. Talking and chattering they shared stories of deliverance. The fellowship was good, God was good, everything was good. No giants, no problems, just a heady taste of freedom.

Having "spoiled" the Egyptians, they were rich beyond their wildest dreams. They showed each other the goodly garments, the gold and silver and precious jewels that their enemies had pressed upon them (Ex. 12:35-36).

Let us pause here. Does this mirror your experience of redemption? Do you remember the day you accepted Jesus as your Deliverer, claiming His death on your behalf? Do you recollect the leap you took from all that was familiar, into the new and exciting unknown? Can you picture again the happy fellowship as you began to travel along the road to freedom with others of like mind? Do you remember sharing your story with them? And do you recollect the joy of finding yourself the possessor of unbelieveable riches—peace of mind and the joy of forgiveness—in fact, all the spiritual riches that are in Christ? Do you remember all that?

Do you remember the visible sense of God with you—as real as that cloud or pillar of fire? Didn't you feel you could almost touch Him? Why, you believed you were ready for *anything!*

The Deep Red Sea

Then suddenly, as suddenly as it all happened to the Children of Israel, it happened to you. The whole scene changed. You realized with a shock of sudden fear that there had been a strange sort of security in bondage. Fears swept away the happy feelings that had filled your heart in those first few glorious days or weeks of liberty, and you even voiced your sentiments, "It was better in Egypt!" This is quite a usual thing to happen to young Christians. You see, what happens is, Pharaoh begins to pursue you. Almost immediately, enraged at your escape, he takes his army and his taskmasters and begins to chase you. Distance always lends enchantment to the view, and suddenly slavery seems a good, safe way of life. The euphoria fades quickly away and there you are, facing the Red Sea.

"Oh God, here I am," you cry. "I'm between the devil and the deep Red Sea. I can't go on, and I can't go back. The future looks impassable and the present is impossible."

You actually could become very angry. Angry at Moses, whoever he or she happens to be. Who was it that disturbed you in the first place? Who brought you out of your bondage security to die in this unsafe wilderness? (Ex. 14:11)

All this is quite, quite normal, so take heart. Moses can't be expected to tell you all that you will possibly meet as you set out on the Christian life. For one thing, he doesn't know!

Moses has his own problems, but he is with you in it. He's going to stick with you if he's any sort of spiritual father at all, and together you will sink or swim through your Red Sea. You might even walk right through on dry ground.

The thing to do is to think back, carefully and realistically to your slavery, and realize it was not better in Egypt. Anything has to be better than that! The fact that Pharaoh is pursuing you does not mean he can catch you, and however loud his soldiers sound as they pound up behind you, God's Presence is in between.

You have to learn to look through the cloud, through the presence of God, at Pharaoh. This way you will get his size. He will certainly be diminished when you filter him that way. God promises, in Romans 6:14, that "sin shall not have dominion over you." Sin need not be your taskmaster once you are delivered. Stand still, and stop jumping up and down in anger about the person or church that got you into all this, and see the salvation of the Lord (Ex. 14:13).

"The Lord shall fight for you" (14:14), and as He protects you from the enemy who is already a defeated foe, He will reassure you that He is with you and that He has some orders you must now obey.

When you face that first obstacle in your new life in Christ and there seems no way through it—in fact it seems just as deep and wide and impassable as the Red Sea was to the Children of Israel—then listen to His command: "Go forward!" (Ex. 14:15) As you obey the impossible, and refuse to go back, as your feet touch the very waters of the impossible command, you will find the waters will divide and you will go through on dry ground. It's a question of faith, not feelings, and that particular Red Sea is one every newly born-again Christian has to face.

The feeling of your immediate escape will diminish, and doubts of all sorts and sizes will set in. "What have I let myself in for? I didn't think I would face this. They never told me that!" you will say. But go forward. Obey without considering those feelings, and you will find that Pharaoh and all his army will be drowned in the very area where he had hoped to see your defeat.

So you are delivered? Good. But you find yourself between the devil and the deep Red Sea? Then go forward, right through it, and you will land safely on the other side of your first big test. Then perhaps you will sing a song like the one in Exodus 15!

Worksheet for Group Study

1. Review what the following characters and things can be said to represent:

Pharaoh	Moses
The plagues	The Passover lamb
The treasures	The Pillar of Cloud and Fire
of Egypt	The deep Red Sea

2. Working in pairs, look up and discuss some further Scriptures that deal with the proposals of Pharaoh used by Satan to prevent people from being delivered.

a. *Sacrifice in bondage.* Nominal Christianity; giving God unacceptable sacrifices (1 Peter 1:18-19).

b. *Stay in sight.* Don't fully commit yourself (Rom. 12:1-2).

c. *Spare your families.* Don't let your family hold you back (Luke 8:19-21; Matt. 10:34-38; Luke 9:59-62).

d. *Sever the cattle.* Let it be a spiritual thing, not a practical one (Ex. 20:24-25; 31:1-11; 35:4-29). What were the goods to be used for?

3. Read the following verse that reminds us of Jesus as the Lamb who has been prefigured in the Passover: John 1:29. Discuss what John the Baptist's words would mean to his audience.

4. In Ephesians 1:18-23, we have a list of the spiritual riches we possess in Christ when we are delivered from Egypt. Make a list of them and discuss them.

5. Share in the group any testimony of the letdown that often follows conversion. Is this a result of relying on feelings instead of facts? Discuss the part a Moses can play to encourage new believers. Look up the commands in Joshua 4:1-9 to go forward. How do you think Joshua felt at this time? Note that God never commands us to wait for our feelings to be right before we obey.

6. Make a list of things a spiritual encourager, or leader, could do to help new converts through their first Red Sea experience.

7. Turn to the victory song of Moses in Exodus 15:1-19.

a. Read it through to yourself.

b. Answer the following questions about verse 2. Moses sang in triumph about three things the Lord was to him personally. They all begin with S, what are they?

c. Gather the attributes of God that Moses spoke of from the following verses, and make a list of them: Exodus 15:3, 6, 7, 11, 13,18.

d. What should be the result of the news of the people's deliverance on those who hear about it? (15:14-16)

8. Prayer

a. Pray for people you know whose love of family or goods is holding them back from full commitment.

b. Thank God for the spiritual riches that are ours in Christ.

c. Pray for new believers who are going through their first Red Sea problem.

d. Pray for your church leaders, that they may nurture babes in Christ and see them grow into full maturity.

e. Pray for yourselves concerning these things, that others may hear of your deliverance and be amazed (v. 15) to His glory.

5

Saved, Satisfied, and Stuck?

Delivered! But what next? To be sure, God did not intend His redeemed people to live forever on the Red Sea shore. The victory had indeed been a great one, and the temptation was to stay and sing about it forever. But God had instructed Moses on the other side of the Red Sea to tell the people to go forward. He did not mean to only go forward to the other side of the problem. I am quite sure He meant them to go forward *ad infinitum*.

To keep on going on is what the Christian life is all about. The Christian life is not a step, or a leap, or even a plunge through the Red Sea. It is a walk.

Not long ago, my husband took up racquetball. Knowing I needed the exercise, I also ventured into the little box that was the court. It seemed a trifle small for the two of us, but it was fun. Having played tennis thousands of years ago, in the days of my youth, I managed quite well. However, being thoroughly out of shape, I found myself running furiously in every direction for about 20 minutes and then suddenly collapsing in a whimpering heap in a corner of the court. My experience reminded me of many young Christians. Starting off with great enthusiasm, they leap frantically around, chasing the ball and running themselves into the ground, ending

53

up beaten in a short span of time. This is not the way to play the game. Watch an expert racquetball player, and you see he paces himself well, knowing just where to put his feet. He even finishes a vigorous game with steps left over. The idea is to plod with God, rather than to race through space. Sitting exhausted in a hotel chair, Vance Havner was asked by a lady if he had enjoyed his tour of Jerusalem. He replied, "Madam, I am 'pooped.' Today I 'ran' where Jesus walked!" Those of us who have been on such tours understand how he felt. But you know, we are not intended to run where Jesus walked. We are to walk with steady, measured tread in the steps of the Master.

The Victorious Christian Life

Where then, are we walking to? We are going to Canaan, the Promised Land. We are going to possess our possessions, to inherit our inheritance. Canaan represents the place God has chosen for us on this earth. Not a physical place, but a spiritual position. This spiritual position or plane of exper-ience, is called "the victorious Christian life."

Only a few days away from your deliverance experience of receiving Jesus as your Saviour, you need to understand two things. First, you need to understand what has already hap-pened to you, and second, you need to understand what should happen next.

When you received Christ by His Spirit, He entered your heart and brought with Him forgiveness (Col. 1:14). He made you a new creature and gave you a new start (2 Cor. 5:17). He promised you that He would never cast you away (John 6:37). You are like a penny standing upright in the palm of His nail-pierced hand. You may fall down, but you can never fall out. The penny is so small, but the hand of the Lord is so large. You are His and He is yours. It's a sort of "exchanged life" as Hudson Taylor described it. You get Him and He gets you. To be sure, He gets the raw end of the deal, but never mind, that is all of grace!

Secondly, you need to start moving and go forward. To

know what to do next, once one has said that vital prayer of commitment, is very important. Becoming a Christian is easy, but being a Christian is another thing.

The exciting possibility is this. It's entirely up to you how long it takes before you start living in Canaan. Knowing what you are supposed to be doing, and then doing it, is up to you to discover from the Word of God. The route from the Red Sea into the land of Canaan should have taken the Children of Israel three weeks to travel. Instead, it took them 40 years, and they never did make it in. Not the generation that escaped from Egypt anyway. Forty years going round in circles in the wilderness, simply because of initial starting problems!

I see very clearly, looking back on my own experience, how very fortunate I was to have a Moses. The girl who led me to Jesus Christ instructed me clearly and concisely on the art of going forward. She did not allow me to be saved, satisfied, and stuck! She showed me how to pray, read the Word, witness, and worship, and provided me with fellowship as well. God blessed me with Jenny's love and spiritual oversight, and this initial authority was very special and important to me.

It's important that you find a spiritually mature person to help you. Someone who loves the Lord and His Word, and will answer all the questions you are bound to need answered.

I hung on every word Jenny spoke to me. I came to respect her, and soon had her on a pedestal, certainly not of her choosing. This is very normal too. We tend to be people worshipers anyway, and when someone has been a help in the spiritual area of our lives, what better person to idolize!

But one thing I did not know, and that is that this is not allowed. God says, "Thou shall have no other gods before me!" It is very important that we keep our spiritual leaders in perspective. We must not place them on pedestals, nor worship them in any form. This does not mean we do not appreciate, pray, and listen to them. We should obey their direction if they are our human shepherds, but we must not place any person in God's place. The pedestal is reserved for Jehovah God, who alone is to be worshiped.

A Collapsed Pedestal

The first bad experience the Children of Israel had in their walk toward Canaan, was with leadership. They very nearly stumbled over this one. Moses fell off his pedestal. Placed on it by the ecstatic people, he managed to keep this elevated position in their affections for precisely three days. Then he fell off into a sand dune, and the trouble began (Ex. 15:22-27).

I remember well the day Jenny fell off the pedestal on which I had placed her. It was as bitter an experience for me as the waters of Marah were for the Children of Israel. I was bitter, simply because I had come to depend on her and she let me down. It was not Jenny's fault. She had never told me to depend on anyone but Jesus, but when you are a young Christian that's hard. It's so much easier to depend on a holy person than a Holy Spirit! It can be a serious thing though. As we look at the incident in the Book of Exodus, we see that the loss of the people's confidence and respect in their human leadership led quite naturally to a loss of confidence in God. That is indeed serious. People will always disappoint you, even someone as wonderful as Moses. Then what will happen to your confidence in God?

The problem is that you are watching a leader learn. No human authority is perfect. This does not lessen their authority, for we must realize that our leaders are learning too.

Moses hadn't had much practice leading thousands of people through a desert. Every minute these murmuring, muttering followers seemed to be saying to him, "You didn't tell us it would be like this!" Moses could easily have answered, "I didn't know! And if I had have known, I might have left you behind in Egypt!"

Just think of Moses' problem. Here he was with thousands of thirsty people on his hands. I wonder if he thought back to his loyal flock in the wilderness. At least they didn't answer him back! They trusted their human shepherd to do the very best for them. It wasn't fair. Why were these people expecting him to provide water? Why did they look at him as if he were a waterfall deliberately damming up the flow!

It is never fair to expect our leaders to supply what God alone can give us. That is not their job. Their job is simply to direct us to our Source of satisfaction, who is the Holy Spirit, and instruct us how to drink.

There is nothing that gets to Stuart and me more, in our positions of leadership, than to have our motives suspected. To be met with suspicious mistrust is a very depressing thing. It is not only a bitter experience for the followers to see their leader fail to produce; it is also a bitter thing for a leader to have his motives misunderstood, and be expected to do the impossible that only God can do.

Moses knew, however, how to make the bitter waters better. The Lord showed him a tree. That's what He always does for me whenever I am on my knees complaining about people complaining. God shows me a tree. He shows me Jesus hanging on it, and I see He's not saying anything at all, except little sentences like "Father, forgive them" or "They know not what they do" or "I thirst." That last one usually gets to me. The Son of God not only thirsted for moisture in His torture of crucifixion, but for the souls of the men and women He died to save. "What shall I drink, Father?" He cried upon the cross. "The bitter waters of Marah," was the reply. The cup of suffering and death! And He did, with never a complaint. And because of all that, we can apply the tree that God shows us in the Bible, the cross of our Lord Jesus Christ, to our bitterness, and have it turned into a sweet experience instead. The Lord will show you a tree, and as you apply the cross to your bitter waters, there will be a healing (Ex. 15:25).

The Bible says that all this happened to test them (v. 25). What was the test? The test was to see if they would depend on Him instead of Moses and Aaron. This does not mean we have scriptural permission to be spiritual mavericks. Our place is under the authority of godly leadership and supervision. But, under that God-given authority, we are supposed to grow, and become supportive and helpful to that very leadership placed over us.

This is the way to spiritual health. To listen and obey Him through His appointed leadership. To grow up so fast we can easily discern our leaders' mistakes, and simply pray for them, support them, and respect them, remembering they too are learning to follow after God.

A Rest at Elim

After Marah, came Elim (v. 27). Twelve wells were found there, one for each tribe, complete sufficiency for everyone's needs. Seventy palm trees provided shade from the heat, and gave them rest from their marching. The psalmist wrote, "Weeping may endure for a night, but joy cometh in the morning" (Ps. 30:5). It was time for respite. Jesus was tempted by the devil 40 days, and afterward the angels came (Matt. 4:11). Elijah, exhausted, ran away from the woman who sought his life. After he could run no more, the angel of the Lord appeared, strengthening him (1 Kings 19:7). After Marah, God will always provide an Elim. A place of spiritual rest and refreshment in the middle of your desert.

Rev. C. I. Scofield wrote, "These bitter waters were in the very path of the Lord's leading, and stand for the trials of God's people, which are educatory and not punitive. The 'tree' [which healed the waters, should remind the Christian that] the cross, which became sweet to Christ as the expression of the Father's will, [can take the bitterness out of all such experiences]. When our Marahs are so taken, we cast the 'tree' into the waters [and blessing and growth follow]." (C. I. Scofield. *The Scofield Reference Bible.* New York: Oxford University Press, 1945, p. 89.)

A child clings to his father's hand as he takes his first tottering steps forward. In love, the father must remove his hand that the child may walk alone. What a ludicrous sight to see a grown man clinging to his father's hand! Yet how many people, having been Christians for years, have never yet let go, and learned to walk as God intended them to walk. They cling, metaphorically speaking, to their pastor's hand. They leave their physical babies in the nursery, yet are spiritual babies themselves. In the same way, the child who begins to walk on his own begins to drink on his own. No longer does he demand that the cup be held to his thirsty lips by his father. The little hands take the cup for themselves and lift the drink to the lips. They are surely still dependent on the father to provide the drink, but they are growing up enough to appropriate the liquid for themselves.

So, go forward to Elim. Find your well and your palm tree. Take a rest and a drink that has been provided by your loving heavenly Father. Camp there for a while, but don't stay too long. Remember, you are not intended to wander round in circles, getting nowhere for 40 years. You are intended to march into the Promised Land. How long will it take you? It depends entirely on which route you take. Listen to and obey the One who drew up the plan and sketched out the way, and you'll pass through the dry desert and arrive in Canaan.

Worksheet for Group Study

1. The Bible has a lot to say about the walk of a Christian. Look up the following verses and paraphrase each verse in your own words.

Romans 6:4	Ephesians 5:2
Romans 8:1, 4	Ephesians 5:15
Romans 13:13	Colossians 2:6
1 Corinthians 3:3	Colossians 4:5
2 Corinthians 4:2	1 Thessalonians 3:6
Ephesians 2:10	1 John 1:6
Ephesians 4:1	1 John 1:7
3 John 4	

2. The Bible has a lot to say about authority. Who gives the rulers of the world authority?

a. Daniel 2:20-21, 37, 44.

b. Read Daniel's interpretation of Nebuchadnezzar's nightmare in Daniel 4:19-37. Write down your deductions from this passage about God giving man authority to rule.

3. What does the Bible say about believers being subject to authority, and what authorities does it talk about? Read the following verses in reference to this:

Ephesians 5:24	1 Peter 5:5
James 4:7	1 Timothy 3:4
Romans 13:1	1 Peter 3:1, 5
Titus 3:1	1 Corinthians 16:16
1 Peter 2:18	1 Peter 2:13-14

Remember: when the law of man contravenes the law of God, we ought to obey God rather than man!

6

Manna in the Morning

Sand in their sandwiches, the monotony of the landscape, thirsty children, and bickering families! No supermarkets or corner grocery stores in the desert. And now no bread! I can't say I blame the Children of Israel for their complaints (Ex. 16:1-8).

God was testing them, and they continued to fail the test (Ex. 16:3). Not only were they murmuring and muttering, but they were looking back. That's a dangerous preoccupation. "Would to God we were back in Egypt. There was plenty to eat there," they said. "Egypt is a better place to die. Why have you brought us out here to deliberately kill us with hunger?" Moses answered them, "Your murmurings are not against us, but against God!" (See verse 7.) If God has put us under a spiritual authority, then we are not to mutter against it. It is God who allows the test to come to all of us, our leaders included. Our murmurings are not really against them, but against the Lord.

What was the essence of their complaint? It was the fact that they had no bread. That seems to be fair enough. You can't live without bread, so it looks as if they had some good reasons for grumbling.

If only we would learn, at the start of our walk with God,

to take our complaint straight to the complaint department. Notice where that is: it is not the pastor's office, or in this case, Moses' tent; it is the very presence of the Lord, for He hears our murmurings (see v. 8).

In chapter 15, the writer recorded that the people were angry with their leaders for not providing water. In chapter 16, we find they are angry that their leaders are not producing bread.

Do we have a right to expect our leaders to produce bread for us? In a way we do. They are there to break the Word of God small enough to nourish us, but we must remember that they are dependent on God to supply it.

The Children of Israel had brought a month's supply of food with them from the land of their captivity. Enough to see them into Canaan, a land flowing with milk and honey. But now, they found themselves wandering round in circles. Two characteristics of a wilderness Christian are hunger and anger. Hunger for bread, and anger at his leadership.

Instead of chiding them to get along into the Promised Land, the God of grace promised His complaining children bread. "I will rain down bread from heaven for you," He promised.

Jesus said, "I am the bread of life" (John 6:35). God rained Jesus on us from heaven one day, and expects us to draw our spiritual sustenance from Him.

He is the living Word who said things to us by His life and actions. Those who read Him aright wrote about Him, and their words are recorded in the Bible. The Scriptures will help us get to know the Bread of Life and teach us how to feed on Him.

Collect It for Yourself

The manna from heaven that God rained on His complaining children is a beautiful picture of the Word of God, the Bread of Life, miraculously provided for spiritually needy men and women.

So then, how does it work? First of all, God gave the

people instructions through Moses (read Exodus 16:14-36).

God told Moses to tell the people about His provision, and then teach them to collect it for themselves. The instructions were detailed; Moses had to collect it for himself as well. In fact, I'm sure he had to be very careful to be a good example, as everyone would want to know if he was going to eat and benefit by it before they dared to try it.

I wonder how many pastors or teachers there are around who tell their congregations how to go and get the manna, but never go and collect any themselves? They are not a good example of obeying the very things they tell others to do. And it shows; they are hungry pastors. They are even wilderness pastors, running round in circles and getting nowhere. The Apostle Paul had something very straightforward to say about that (Rom. 2:21).

But even though Moses and Aaron collected their own manna, I want you to notice they did not collect it for everybody else. They told them it was God's provision, and instructed them to go and collect it themselves, and how to digest it so it would benefit them. The choice of action was theirs.

Just imagine if Moses had had to get up early each day to collect manna for every man, woman, and child. He would have had to set his sundial at 1:00 A.M. and then some!

Do you know how good God's manna is? Do you believe Jesus and His Word can satisfy that craving within you? Are you satisfied? Or do you complain about your minister, who you expect to do the collecting, and spoon-feed you all your life? Maybe some of you reckon that that's what you are paying him for.

According to the Apostle Paul (Eph. 4:11-12), the pastor-teacher is there to teach and train *you*, "the saints" (which is just another name for believers), to do the work of the ministry.

Have you learned how to collect your manna, or is the Bible still a complete mystery to you? Are you frightened of it? Is it a big dark house that you are reluctant to enter?

Day by Day

The illustration in Exodus 16 gives us some guidelines for studying the Bible. First of all, they were instructed by God to collect the manna daily. Every day a little manna. Not just on the Sabbath. In fact, the Sabbath was the only day they were not to collect it! Just imagine if your pastor announced it was against God's law to conduct Bible study on the Sabbath, but that you had to conduct it daily for yourself. I almost wish the pastors of well-blessed churches would say that sometimes, and watch what would happen.

Some of you may say, "I've been wandering around for years being bitter at my pastor for not feeding me. I'm so hungry I've a terrible case of spiritual malnutrition. I've known somehow I should put all that energy I use complaining into collecting manna, but I just don't know when or how to start!"

The best way to begin is to begin. It's better just to start anywhere than not start at all. I suggest the New Testament. Maybe you could read some of Paul's advice to new Christians from the Epistles. Or start by collecting information about Jesus, the Bread of Life, from one of the Gospels. "All Scripture is given by inspiration of God, and is profitable for doctrine, for reproof, for correction, for instruction in righteousness. That the man of God may be perfect, thoroughly furnished unto all good works" (2 Tim. 3:16-17). So it really doesn't matter where you start to read—it's all inspired and inspirational. Ask yourself questions as you collect a little every day. Questions such as, "Who is writing this?" "Who are the characters involved?" "What are they doing, and why?" "What is the reaction of the crowd?" Or if you are in an instructional passage of Scripture, ask, "What does this say?" "What does it say to me?" "What does it say to my family, my society, or my country?" Go to your pastor, and ask him how to collect the manna of the Word of God and, if he can't tell you, go and find someone who can.

If we were short of physical bread, I know I would leave

no stone unturned till I found someone who could tell me how to get some. How much more should we be concerned with food for our souls.

Secondly, the Children of Israel were told to collect the manna early. We can apply this two ways. We can apply it to our children, or ourselves, if we are young in years. The writer of Ecclesiastes 12:1 stated that if we can establish a habit of collecting manna in the days of our youth, then we will continue to remember our Creator when we are old. If you have children, find some creative Bible readings for them. (I suggest "Scripture Union Bible Reading Notes," 1716 Spruce Street, Philadelphia, Pennsylvania 19103; or "Daily Readings for Young Christians," from David C. Cook Foundation, Cook Square, Elgin, Illinois 60120.) It was the Israelite father's job to collect the manna for the family, and also to teach his children to collect it for themselves. Their questions must be answered. Your child who wants to know what God is like, and how he can know Him, has only one person to ask, and that's you. Do you know the answers? When your little one is trying to collect manna, don't withhold it from him. The writer of Deuteronomy 6:7 stated, "And thou shalt teach them [that is, the words of God] diligently unto thy children, and shalt talk of them when thou sittest in thine house, and when thou walkest by the way, and when thou liest down, and when thou risest up."

Thirdly, the Children of Israel were told to assimilate the manna while it was fresh. It would not keep for another day. It would go stale. Some Christians I know are living on manna they collected 30 years ago. It's so stale it has even become obnoxious, just as God said His desert manna would, if it was not put to use (Ex. 16:20).

"Oh," some of you may say, "I tried that Bible reading thing, but it went off on me and I went off on it!" Surely it did, because you didn't collect it new every morning. It was intended to be put to immediate use. This could only happen when it was thoroughly digested. To read the Scriptures and to digest the Scriptures are totally different things. Just as seeing and perceiving are different, or hearing and really listening. God told Joshua to meditate on His Word (Josh. 1:8). The word means to "chew over," rather like a cow chews the cud, so that its body can put it to use. It's not going to benefit us one bit to simply read our little passage as if it is a lucky charm to keep the evil spirits away. We must mix it with faith, chew it over thoroughly, and swallow it. We need to accept it into our very heart, and then act on it. We will then find the strength will be there for the obedience God demands from us.

Collecting manna early can also mean that a new Christian needs to learn to study the Bible as soon as he or she becomes a believer. You can learn to collect it early in your Christian experience. The Apostle Peter wrote, "As newborn babes, desire the sincere milk of the word, that ye may grow thereby: if so be ye have tasted that the Lord is gracious" (1 Peter 2:2-3). There is milk and there is meat in the Bible. There is every diet necessary in the Scriptures, from baby food to a menu for adult appetites. A babe can learn quickly to feed itself. And children don't wait till they are grown men to use a knife and fork!

Collecting manna early can also speak to us of getting ourselves out of bed at the beginning of God's new gift of another day. "Before the sun is up" (see v. 21), God said. Have you ever collected heavenly manna before the sun was up? Before the heat of the day? The cool of the day and the manna of God will prepare you and give you strength to face the monotonous sand dunes that span your horizon, or the enemies that lurk around the next corner of your journey of life.

"Give us food!" the Children of Israel screamed at Moses and Aaron. "Go and get it yourselves!" they answered. "Gather it according to your eating" (v. 21). There is enough to satisfy the most ravenous wilderness Christian. God always has bread for His people. He has promised, as our Shepherd, to lead us into green pastures, and teach us to lie down there. The way a shepherd teaches a sheep to lie down is quite simple, for the sheep is an animal that only lies down when its stomach is full. This shows it is satisfied. Then it can rest beside the still waters. It does not run around bleating and complaining about its shepherd. Its shepherd leads the flock into green grass, and the sheep's responsibility is to eat! The shepherd cannot eat for the sheep.

I believe the antidote for criticism is manna. Show me a complaining Christian, and I'll show you one who is not collecting his daily food. "Give us this day our daily bread," Jesus instructed His followers to pray. Then when it is given, take it and eat it!

When Sunday Comes

I mentioned at the start of this chapter, that the people were instructed not to gather any manna on the Sabbath, for there would be none to gather "in the field" (v. 25). God did not want them to have to do that. So they had to "lay up" enough for their day of rest. When the Sabbath came, they could simply share it with each other and enjoy it together. It was one day of the week the bread was to be provided and preserved for the whole family. It was to be in the tent, not in the field.

I am quite sure from my own experience that if I faithfully collect and absorb my daily manna, when Sunday comes, that which I do not collect for myself, but is laid up for me by my spiritual head, is all the more enjoyable. I approach worship with a totally new attitude. I enter my church fellowship with exciting anticipation. What the preacher says makes sense— perhaps I have been eating around the same patch of ground he is working on! My hunger or appetite is there, of course, for daily hunger requires daily bread, but now, just for once, it is someone else's responsibility to feed me. It is the Lord's Sabbath. I rest from my labor of collecting, and I absorb my spiritual leader's food. If I come starving to my Sunday worship, I shall simply be sick, for how can a shrunken stomach digest such a sudden meal?

Each of us needs a fellowship of believers to belong to. Insights shared from other people's collecting are vital to give us balance and help. Find a place where the manna is broken well. Make sure your pastor and teachers believe, "This is the bread which the Lord hath given you to eat" (16:15), and are faithfully preaching it. Don't absorb strange food that isn't the inspired, infallible Word of God. Don't look for a change of diet, some modern new recipe that purports to have superceded God's Scriptures as set forth in the Old and New Testaments. Find a fundamental Bible-believing "tent," and be there on the Sabbath to share and eat together. This is the Lord's command.

There was a small group of people that didn't think this was at all necessary. "And it came to pass, that there went out some of the people on the seventh day for to gather, and they found none" (v. 27). God was rightly frustrated at their arrogance and disobedience.

In my experience, I have met such people, and I must confess they irritate me too. There is a danger of new Christians who, having been encouraged to gather manna for themselves, can decide they do not need any tent fellowship on the Sabbath. They can become proud, independent, and disobedient to God's command, "Not forsaking the assembling of ourselves together" (Heb. 10:25). They have discovered how to gather their daily manna, and they think they can do without others sharing their food with them one day of the week. This is another form of immaturity. I can't think of anything that gets to me more than members of a church who become so holy and proud of the way they are daily collecting all that manna, that they feel they are beyond needing that essential "tent sharing" once a week. They too begin to complain about their pastor. This time they are not starving Christians, because they are feeding themselves, but they are surely self-righteous Christians, who need to be reminded of something. God has commanded every man to go to his tent of fellowship on His holy day, and those who insist on going out and collecting their own will find none. Why? It's in the tents; that's where God has ordained the food will be obtained, and that is where we are to digest it, one day a week.

I have met groups of young Christians who feel they do not need to identify with a body of believers. They meet and study the Bible, or listen to tapes, in splendid isolation. But the structure of the authority of the church, as laid down in the Epistles, is missing. To those who go out on their own on the Sabbath, God would say, as He did to the children of Israel: "How long refuse ye to keep My commandments and My laws?" (v. 28)

We need the discipline of the church body. We need to be in God's house on the Sabbath, sharing the manna we have collected and laid up for that day with others, instead of deciding that those immature people and these shallow shepherds can't teach us anything. We need to submit ourselves to the authority of their leadership. Be very, very careful how you accuse the annointed leaders whom the Lord has placed over you. You will be held accountable for your grumblings.

In summary, we must learn early to collect our daily manna for ourselves. Our God-appointed shepherds should instruct us carefully how to do this, and we are to gather in our tents once a week to share together that which has been laid up for us by our leaders. This is a commandment of the Lord. We are to stop complaining against Moses and Aaron, for our complaints are really against God—He hears our mumblings and mutterings and is distressed with us! In Numbers 14:27, the Lord complains about complaining: "How long shall I bear with this evil congregation, which murmur against Me?"

There is no way we can enter into that land of promised victory in our Christian experience, if we insist on doing these things. God has said so, and we will simply spend 40 years wandering round and round in ever decreasing circles till we die in our desert—still grumbling, still mumbling and still hungry! So get up before the sun rises, collect your daily bread, and obey the commands and laws of God. Be in your tent faithfully on the Sabbath, sharing and resting. Respect your human and fallible guides, knowing a divine and infallible God has invested them with His authority. This way you will be well on your way to Canaan—and with a full stomach.

Worksheet for Group Study

Here is a practical plan for one week of manna for your spiritual needs.

Monday. Read some of Paul's advice to new Christians, in Philippians 4:1-9. Underline all the *commands* you can find in this passage. Pray to God, asking Him to help you keep them.

Tuesday. Read John 4:1-42 and write down all the things Jesus did in this incident that we need to do for others as we witness to them. Pray that God will show us one individual we can talk to about Him.

Wednesday. Read Luke 8:22-25. Ask yourself these questions: Who is writing this? Who is it about? What is happening? Why? When? What does this show me of Jesus? What does it show me about myself?

Thursday. Read Romans 8. Underline all the *promises*. Pray that God will help your unbelief. Pray that others who need the promises will appropriate them.

Friday. Read 1 Corinthians 15:58. Write down 10 things this verse tells you. Search diligently, and you will find them! Follow the same procedure for 2 Timothy 2:15 and James 1:12.

Saturday. Read James 1:25 and memorize it. Why? Read Psalm 119:9-11. That's why!

Sunday. Read the Book of Ephesians right through without stopping. Pray about the verses that were most meaningful to you.

1. Take your calendar and mark in a time each day this coming week that you will collect your manna.

2. Share with each other in your group helpful ideas you know about to use in a quiet time.

3. Make a list of hindrances to your quiet time. Pray about it in pairs.

Write a personal letter to God, asking Him to meet with you on a regular basis.

7

Speak to the Rock

Our home in Wisconsin is located in a beautiful country district, and for this reason, we are dependent on a well for water. One day, like the woman in the song, I found myself seeking. Our well was dry, and I had to telephone the local well diggers. After an involved explanation on my part, they told me how much per foot it would cost to drill deeper. They couldn't tell me how deep it would have to be, because they would have to drill until they found that new water vein. It was a costly enterprise to find the source.

Man can survive without food for quite a while, but to live without water is another thing. When you live in a desert, you are continually reminded that you need a drink. God's people required a source of water to survive in the wilderness, and so do we. The desert of the world in which we live is such that our spirits cry out continually for refreshment. (See Ex. 17:1-7.)

God told Moses that He would stand before him on this special rock in Horeb, and that he was to strike it with his rod. Moses' rod represented God's authority, while the rock depicted Jesus Christ, who was to be smitten on the cross. When the rock was smitten, the water was released. The miracle of the gushing water can be a beautiful picture of the

One who was to be the Source of Israel's survival, the blessed Holy Spirit.

God wants us to have that continual craving for Him met and satisfied. He is the Source of our satisfaction, but we must always remember what a costly enterprise it was for God to "dig deeper." It wasn't until the Roman soldiers nailed the Son of God on the cross that He finished the work of supplying our redemption.

God was drawing pictures in the sand again, and Israel learned another lesson. Do you get the picture too? Sinful man must come to the smitten Rock, and in his desperate need, receive the Spirit—the Water of Eternal Life. That is the beginning.

Our Needs Supplied

From that point on, we need to daily gather our manna and drink of the Spirit! What does that mean? It means that as we daily speak to the risen Rock about our thirsts, the Spirit will continue to supply us. Perhaps we are thirsty for *companionship*. Maybe you are the only Christian in your family, and you feel so alone. Don't say "I'm the only one." Start saying, "I'm the first one." As you wait for your loved ones to put their trust in Jesus, begin to trust the Rock to supply your need of companionship through the Spirit. His name is "the Comforter" and He will be the One called alongside to help, just as He promised you in John 14:26. You may be alone, but you need never be lonely.

Perhaps you are thirsty for *excitement* or change in your schedule. Your life seems so dull, drab, and monotonous. You have really been able to identify with all these people wandering round in circles, and getting nowhere for 40 years. Except in your case, it feels like 80 years! "Speak to the Rock," and the Spirit will supply your need. Do you remember that in Genesis 1:2, the writer stated there was once a situation without form. It was void. Just a deep hole. Nothingness. Blah! You couldn't even see anything, because darkness was on the face of the deep. Is that a little like a description of your life?

Even though God is your Father and Christ is your Saviour? Well, look what is stated in the verse: the Spirit of God moved, or brooded, on the face of that whole situation. God began to speak, and the Spirit supplied His intentions: new light, new life, new love, all came to being in that monotonous landscape. Everyday something new that had never happened before happened. That can be your experience too.

Speak to the Rock about your need and God will do something He has never done before for anyone else, and He will do it every day. He will not perhaps transport you from your environment, but He will touch your situation with His creative genius. Being the Originator of all creativity, He won't get stuck for a new idea for your dull landscape. He doesn't copy something He has done for someone else. Each creative act is unique because you are unique. Ask Him for a genesis in your "verse 2" life, and you'll see it will be very, very good. He will turn the monotonous into the momentous.

Perhaps you are thirsty for *appreciation*. No one really understands how hard you work, and you never seem to receive a word of thanks. Maybe no one even notices the effort it takes to do that insignificant duty in church. They don't appear to think it really matters if you turn up or not at the group meeting or at the club. They never ask you to help, or if they do, they forget to notice it or to repay you. You're so thirsty for someone to need you; you need to be needed!

Speak to the Rock; He needs you. He's never given life to an unimportant person. Each of you is significant. He notices, and He watches you work; He always says "thank you," for in 1 Corinthians 13:5, Paul wrote, "Love has good manners" (PH). (See also Heb. 6:10.) God asks you to do something very special for Him; He asks you to be His ambassador down here, representing the King (2 Cor. 5:20). Yes, little you! He trusts you with messages to the foreigners you live among, and He trusts you to represent Him faithfully. How privileged can you be? If you aim to please Him instead of trying to please the church, then His "Well done" will be the only appreciation you will be looking for.

Perhaps you are thirsty for the power to be different. The power to *change* and stop doing some of the things you wish you could stop doing, and to start doing things you know you should. Speak to the Rock. The Spirit will make the power you need operative in your life.

Battling Amalek

Maybe you want to ask, "What do you mean, Jill, by speaking to the Rock?" Well, I'm really talking about prayer; the speaking part of our relationship with the Source of our spiritual survival that releases the power we need to be Christlike. When you are battling with your own personal thirst, you need to speak in prayer to the Rock. The very next part of our text, Exodus 17:8-16, illustrates this beautifully.

As soon as Israel had been instructed about the source of their help, Amalek came and fought with them. It's just as if God teaches us a lesson and then takes us on a field trip to test it out. It's like learning driving theory in the classroom and then being told it's time to get into the car. Theory and practice must go together. We need opportunities to work out what God is working in (Phil. 2:13). Amalek was strong, and didn't like God's people; in fact, he was their avowed enemy. Amalek can be to us a picture of the "flesh," or self. The Bible tells us God vowed He would have war with Amalek throughout all generations (v. 16). Selfishness must have no part in our lives once we are delivered. At the start of World War II, England declared war on Germany. Soon other nations acknowledged that war had been declared, and joined in. They became England's allies. Once we recognize God has declared war on selfishness, it behooves us to join in. We need to become allied with God in His declaration of hostilities against the enemy, Amalek, on the battlefield of our own hearts.

One of the things you will discover as a new Christian is that self does not die the moment you receive Christ. He may be momentarily stunned, but he does not die. It is often a complete surprise to new Christians to have the first rosy hue of their newborn experience die away, and be faced with an enemy like Amalek. Selfishness just isn't expected in their new life, and when Amalek confronts them, the surprise of his ugly appearance can result in overwhelming defeat. The Children of Israel were well into their new experience, and then came Amalek and fought with them. I believe he took them by surprise. Until the day you die, you will be met by Amalek. To help you recognize him, here is a word portrait of your enemy taken from Ruth Paxson's marvelous book, *Life on the Highest Plane* (Chicago: Moody Press, 1928):

Self-will. "We have turned every one to his own way." The flesh wants its own way and is determined to have it even if it defies and disobeys God and overrides others. "I will" is the alphabet out of which self fashions its language of life.

Self-centeredness. "The old man" feeds upon himself. He is the beginning and the end. Life presents little that interests or affects him, except as it relates to himself. He is the center of the world in which he lives and moves, and he always looks out for Number One.

Self-assertion. "The old man" believes that every one is as interested in him and as fascinated by him as he himself is, so he protrudes and projects himself into the sight, hearing, and notice of others continually. He monopolizes conversation and the theme is always "I," "my," and "mine." He walks with a swagger and expects the world to stop work and look at him. And he never dreams how offensive his self-importance is to others.

Self-depreciation. "The old man" is very versatile and sometimes it suits his purpose better to clothe his pride in a false humility. He curls up in his self-depreciation and shirks a lot of hard work which other people have to do. He magnifies his littleness and feebleness to his own advantage, yet with strange inconsistency he resents others taking seriously his professed estimate of himself and treating him accordingly.

Self-conceit. "The old man" lives so much in himself

that he does not know how big the world is in which he lives, and how many other really intelligent people there are in it, so he has little regard for the opinions of others, especially if contrary to his own. He looks with proud and supercilious pity upon those less favored and gifted than himself.

Self-love. "The old man" loves himself supremely, one might say almost exclusively. He loves God not at all and his human love for others is tainted more or less with selfishness, jealousy, envy, or impurity. Indeed, "the old man" makes an idol of himself which he not only loves but worships.

Self-indulgence. "The old man" eats, drinks, and is merry. For him to want anything is equivalent to having it. He pampers and coddles himself; he can even indulge his extravagant, fleshly appetites while others starve to death before his eyes.

Self-pleasing. "The old man" chafes under discomfort and deprivation and is grumpy and peevish unless everything in the life of his day ministers to his real or imagined needs. He lives unto only one person, whose name is, not surprisingly, self.

Self-seeking. "The old man" is on a quest: he is after whatever will advance the cause of self. He seeks with feverish ambition and activity praise, position, power, prominence; and anything that checks his gaining them is attributed to others.

Self-pity. His love for himself often creates within "the old man" rebellion against his circumstances or relationships; he exaggerates his own possible suffering, discomfort, or sorrow, and makes himself and others miserable by his habitual murmuring.

Self-sensitiveness. "The old man" is extremely hard to live with because he is covered with wounds and is continually being hurt afresh. He is not very companionable because usually he is dissolved in tears, shrouded in silence, or enjoying a pout.

Self-defense. "The old man" is very jealous of his rights and busy avenging his wrongs. He indulges freely in lawsuits. In his pursuit of his own vindication and justification in cases of disagreement and estrangement with others, he is blinded by his own sin.

Self-trust. "The old man" is very self-confident and feels no need of one wiser and stronger than himself. Trusting in his own powers and resources, he is prone to say, "Though all men shall deny Thee, yet will not I."

Self-sufficiency. The self-confidence of "the old man" fosters an egotistical, smug self-satisfaction which leaves him stagnant. He has neither desire nor sense of need for anything beyond what he already possesses.

Self-consciousness. "The old man" never forgets himself: wherever he goes he casts a shadow of himself before. He is constantly occupied with photographing himself and developing the plates. He is chained to himself and as he walks one hears the clank of the chains. He is often morbidly self-introspective.

Self-exaltation. "The old man" is absorbed in his own excellencies: he overestimates himself and his abilities: he thirsts for admiration and praise and he thrives on flattery. He secretly worships at the shrine "Self," and he wishes others to do so publicly.

Self-righteousness. "The old man" loves to dress himself in the garments of morality, benevolence and public-spiritedness. He even patronizes the church and often assists in drives for raising money for philanthropic and religious purposes, heading the list of donors with a handsome gift. He keeps a double entry account book—both with the church and with the world, and expects a reward both on earth and in heaven.

Self-glorying. Perhaps "the old man" resents this plain delineation of himself as he really is, and thinks the condemnation too sweeping. Immediately he begins to enumerate his good qualities, his amiableness, geniality, tolerance, self-control, sacrificial spirit, and other virtues.

In doing so, he takes all the credit to himself for what he is, exhibiting ill-concealed pride and vanity.

You Have to Resist

To know and recognize your enemy is half the battle! Joshua took his fighting forces and engaged the enemy in a terrible fight. There are some people who say that God will fight for you. All you do is let Him. Don't do anything! Well I don't buy that. You have to do one thing. You have to resist the devil. The Scripture says, "Resist the devil and he will flee from you" (James 4:7). That's an order, and it involves work. The word resist means to "actively oppose." Are you trying to tell me Joshua didn't put out any effort that memorable day? Read the story in Exodus 17, and then tell me he didn't do anything. Joshua was fighting, all right, but his battle in the valley was balanced by the watch kept by Moses, Aaron, and Hur on the mountaintop.

The symbol of the authority of the God of Israel was in Moses' hand. As he held the rod above the whole situation, he spoke to the Lord about Joshua and his battle. Joshua was fighting, but the God of Israel fought for him. Over and over again, we read these words, "And God fought for Israel." But whenever you read this, you will see that Israel was fighting too. The battle was won before they began, because they knew they had the Lord God of Hosts on their side, but the battle still had to be fought. You have to meet the enemy and engage in the struggle. You have to stand your ground and refuse to move. There is no victory without a battle. But with the Lord God of Israel on your side, you can know that victory is secured. You can know, even as you see the enemy approaching, that he is beaten. God is stronger than Amalek. You're not, but He will strengthen you as you fight, until you are! Remember that the Apostle John wrote, "greater is He that is in you, than he that is in the world" (1 John 4:4).

You have to believe the rod of God is held over you. God is in control. The authority of His Word says, "Sin shall not have dominion [or enjoy the mastery] over you" (Rom. 6:14). Self need not win the battle. God promises that you can, but God also commands you to fight for it. We have to appropriate the forces available. Our part is to say "No" to selfishness, and seek a Moses, an Aaron, and a Hur to sit on the mountain and pray for us. I have experienced winning as my prayer partners have engaged in fervent prayer on my behalf, and weakening when they weary. That's why two or three prayer partners are a good idea. When one gets tired, the other two hold up his hands.

The New Testament records Christ's exhortation (Matt. 18:18-20) to gather together with two or three believers to pray. Joshua knew what it was to watch from the mountain for others, but he also knew he needed prayer help when it was his turn to fight. So when Amalek comes, you are going to need reminding of God's authority over sin, selfishness, and Satan. His Word is His bond, and He promised the battle will be won, but you will need help. You can also help others who are fighting Amalek. There is no greater privilege than holding up one's hands to heaven and claiming God's mastery for a Joshua in the valley. Ask God to remind the strugglers in the valley of His sovereignty and the potential victory that can be claimed. The authority of His Word should be used to hold back Satan's forces from the scene. However young a Christian may be, he is called to the ministry of prayer.

Starve Him Out

God didn't tell Israel to play with Amalek, or pamper him, or ignore him, or make an alliance or truce with him. There was to be no compromise. He was to be put away. Does that mean we can kill selfishness? No! We will never be totally free until the day of our funeral. In fact, as far as those of us who die are concerned, it won't be our funeral at all—it will be the old nature's. It will be our birth into heaven and his death. One day he will be put away just as Satan will be. Until that time, God promises we can live as if our old self is dead already. We can pay no attention to his needs. We can drive him out of our territory. But how? One way is to begin to starve him out.

I heard an illustration once of a bird called the cuckoo. It always lays its eggs in another bird's nest. When little Mrs. Birdie, the nest's owner, comes along, she doesn't bother counting the eggs. She has to work her feathers to the bone hatching this huge monstrosity of an egg, this foreign nature she finds in her nest. When hatched, it begins to steal the worms Mrs. Birdie finds, and soon grows big enough to tip the starving chicks out. Thereafter the cuckoo reigns supreme. The two natures in that one nest picture our condition. In our lives, we have selfishness and Jesus, by His Spirit, living within. The nature which prospers and grows, eventually gaining dominion, depends on us to feed it. If Amalek had stayed put in his walled city, Joshua could have tried starving him out. That's one method of dealing with him, and you could try it too. Make sure you are feeding God's nature, not self.

As it happened, Amalek attacked Israel, and Israel had to stand firm and resist, then counterattack with prayer to drive him off. Likewise, you can always stand firm and say "No." Oh yes, you can. God says so. However weak it sounds, even a whispered "No" will be sufficient to turn the devil away. You can say "No" just as easily as you can say "Yes." You have to say it without feeling "No," that's all. Whatever you do, don't trust your feelings in a battle; do what you are told, and not what you feel. Actively oppose Amalek by saying "No" to self and "Yes" to God, and then act as if you mean it. The feelings will follow.

So speak to the Rock about your own needs: The needs for companionship, excitement, appreciation, and the power to be different. Speak also to the Rock about your brother's needs in the valley in the heat of the battle. Learn to pray on his behalf, claiming God's authority over hostile situations. But learn to fight as well. Ask God to help you to hate what He hates—Amalek, the picture of selfishness—and determine either to starve him out or resist him face to face. Speak to the Rock and He will fight for you and supply your needs.

Worksheet for Group Study

The Rock

1. *The Old Testament.*

a. In Deuteronomy 32:4, the Rock is identified for us. Who is He?

b. In Deuteronomy 32:28-30 what is said about Israel's enemies, concerning their source of support?

c. In 2 Samuel 23:3, David makes a statement concerning the Rock. What is it?

2. *The New Testament.* Here we see the Rock represents Christ as well. Read 1 Corinthians 10:4 to see the Rock identified.

a. What are we told in Ephesians 2:20?

b. What does Romans 9:32-35 add to our information?

c. Read Daniel 2:34 and note an Old Testament fact that will become a future reality. See also Matthew 21:44.

After gathering this *information* and reading the Bible's *interpretation,* it is time for *application.*

3. *The Smitten Rock.* In Matthew 26:31, "I will smite the shepherd," Christ quotes from Zechariah 13:7. The smitten Rock produces the flow of the Spirit, to sustain and satisfy God's people. The water of life is necessary for Canaan living.

Look up and read John 4:1-14. Jesus claimed His ability to impart living water to satisfy the soul. Read John 7:37-39 and identify the living water.

4. The Holy Spirit is holy. Therefore, He cannot abide with selfishness. In fact, He cannot be satisfied unless war is declared on Amalek—a picture of our selfish nature.

a. Where did Amalek come from (Gen. 36:12), and what was his nature?

b. Read Deuteronomy 25:17-19, and answer these questions:

      (1) How does Amalek attack us?

      (2) When does Amalek attack us?

      (3) What is God's command to Israel, and us?

c. Write out God's intentions for Amalek, as described in Exodus 17:16. An example of a Christian who has not declared war on Amalek and is allowing himself to be overcome in battle, is found in James 4:4-7.

d. Discuss and apply this teaching about Amalek to your own life. Pray about all of this. Spend some time in quietness, thinking about God's intentions and provisions for you.

8

The Schoolmaster

Religion is as universal as man who, being a spiritual being, cannot help himself believing in something outside his frame of reference. That's what makes him different from the animals. The animals do not kneel to pray, or ours doesn't anyway! But there is an innate something built into man's makeup that says, "There is an entity outside of me that I need to know, and need to reach out to." You'll find that sense of belief in another being or beings that demand our worship wherever you go in the world. Now you might say, "What about the Chinese Communists? They don't believe in a superior being, and they don't worship anything." Oh, but they do; they simply worship the state.

Religion gives the idea of God; that's what religion is all about. It says, "Hey, there—did you know that God IS?" Theology collects all the ideas about this Being and seeks to order them and give them content. Then it indexes them for us to examine. That's what theology is all about; it is a study of God. Religion gives the idea of God, and theology collects the facts and records them.

Not all religions have been able to do this. Only in a few highly developed ones do you find systematic tabulations. That's why some religions of the past never lasted. They didn't have any doctrine. The thoughts or words about what God said weren't preserved or passed on to others. They didn't survive because there wasn't anyone to think through the things they were saying about their ideas of God.

Brahmanism, Buddhism, Judaism, Islamism, and Christianity are what we call the higher systems of religious thought, and they all have a theology. These are some of the great thought systems of our world. All the recorded religions believe in a Divine Being, and in man's relationship to Him, even though they conceive of Him in different ways.

The problem facing you and me is to determine which one in this array of beliefs is right. Is everybody a little bit right? Or is one religion *all* right? It can be a puzzle. Not only can it be a puzzle, but it can result in complete confusion for many people, because into the great thought systems that have been around for a long time, have come new thoughts and ideas as well.

If you go back to the beginning of history, you can read about man's involvement in animism, fetishism, polytheism, henotheism, pantheism, deism, etc. Most of these primitive people worshiped spirits. They didn't worship an object; the object simply represented the spirit who lived within it. For example, in animism, the idol in front of which a man came to worship could have been a tree. The tree would represent the spirit that lived inside it, or the sun would represent the spirit that sent the sun. This innate sense that there was a spirit world seems to have been around as long as man has been around. These ancient people believed in God as a Spirit and they made an effort to reach out to Him. Now the problem with all these religions, bar Christianity and Judaism, was that they were all man's ideas about God. It was like a man building a tower to heaven to get near enough to see and understand what this Great Being was like. Men actually *did* build a tower with this in mind at a place called Babel. Babel means confusion, and that's where we shall all end up if we depend, as they did, on our own intelligence and scientific findings to try and figure God out!

Christianity claims that God has taken the initiative and revealed Himself, so it is not a question of man's speculative philosophy, but of revealed theology. God has said, "I will tell you what I'm like, I will tell you what I think, I will tell you how I feel, and I will show you what I'll do! I will even come down and become one of you so you can understand Me. I will speak with a man's voice, I will live in a man's house, I will eat man's food; I will meet you face to face." Read John 14:8-9, and notice that Jesus Christ said exactly these things to Philip.

There is no religion in the world, apart from Christianity, that claims God became man and yet kept His divine nature. There is also no other religion in the world that tells of a God-Man's death and resurrection. How did God tell the people who were alive in Old Testament times about Himself and His intentions? Among other things, He used a man's voice.

Climbing the Mountain

If I were God, and I had made you and wanted to talk to you, how should I do it? I'd probably use a human sort of voice that you would be familiar with and therefore understand. And so it is no problem to me to realize that God spoke with a voice. In Deuteronomy 4:36, the writer states that "Out of the heaven He made thee to hear His voice, that He might instruct thee"; and "Thou heardest His words." What did He say? What was the doctrine of this theology that He told Moses to write down? Well now, that is quite a story. It involves poor old Moses doing some energetic mountain climbing. It wasn't just what God said to him that's so interesting, but where He said what He said (Ex. 19).

First of all, God called Moses up to the top of Mount Sinai. He got to the top of the mountain, and God said, "Now I want you to go down to the bottom of the mountain, and tell the people that tomorrow you are going to meet with Me." So Moses wended his weary way back down to the bottom of the mountain. He got the people together and said, "Listen to me! Tomorrow is going to be a very special day. You know that cloud that's been following us all this way? Well, that same manifestation of the presence of God is actually going to cover this mountain and I am supposed to go up into it and meet with God. Then I'll come back and tell you what He said."

So all the people got cleaned up and sanctified, and ready to meet God. The next day, Moses climbed to the top of the mountain again. And God came down, the mountain quaked, there was fire and great shaking of the ground, and the people were petrified. Moses, I'm quite sure, was quaking too, but he must have had a fantastic sense of exhilaration and anticipation. He was all ready to find out God's instructions when the Lord said, "Moses, I want you to go down there and warn those people not to touch the mountain, because if they do, they are going to be killed!" Now, as you can appreciate, Moses was somewhat pooped by now; three times up and down Sinai isn't like jogging round a desert track!

And so, understandably, he said weakly, "The people can't come up to Mount Sinai. You and I both told them that bounds are set about the mount" (v. 23). But the Lord said, "Away, get thee down" and there was nothing to do but to obey.

Why all the hassle? I think God was trying to teach Moses and the people how dangerous it is to approach the living God, and how important His Words must be. They are surely worth the effort of climbing a mountain three times in two days. If the sight of Him made a mountain quake, what should we do with a sound from Him? How awful that must be. Do we today approach the Words His voice spoke in that same attitude of fear and reverence? I think not!

God's Words are the most marvelous and frightening things in His world, yet some of us cannot remember the Ten Commandments, and most of us wouldn't even walk two blocks to ask about them, much less exert ourselves like Moses did.

Let me give you a definition of a law before we continue: law is a rule laid down for the guidance and instruction of an intelligent being, by an intelligent being. We are made with the ability to know that God exists. So if we can exert our intelligence to understand the rules laid down for our guidance by this supernatural intelligent Being, then we are going to find a way of living, a philosophy that will guide us into making intelligent sense out of life.

It's Time for School

Remember, that just before this event, the Children of Israel had come from bondage to freedom. They'd been delivered from hard labor into life. It had been like a birth experience, and now they had a new existence. Some of you are like that. You've come from the bondage and slavery of Egypt and received a new start. It's been like a new birth, and you have begun to grow, for all babies grow.

After babies grow into children, it's time to go to school. That time had come for the Children of Israel. God was about to introduce His children to their schoolmaster. The name of their teacher was Mr. Law. Do you remember your first teacher? I think all of us do. I remember mine had a big nose! I don't remember anything else about her, but that nose seemed to fill my world for weeks.

Those of you who have children will recall asking your child after that first day of school, "What is your teacher like?" That's the thing that has been occupying their mind for weeks. They have been wondering, "Will he be welcoming? Will he be cruel? Will he understand when I get Ds all the time?" You know, that sort of thing.

Mr. Law was Israel's teacher's name (Gal. 3:23-24). He was not very nice; he was a hard schoolteacher. In fact, he was very difficult indeed, and Israel decided they did not like going to school! Since that time, man in general has not liked going to school when Mr. Law is the schoolteacher.

Notice, the Law was given to a delivered people. Now this is very important. The Law was not given to them to get them out of Egypt. The Law was given to them after they had been delivered by the Passover lamb. Today, people are making a big mistake. They think the Law was given to get them out of Egypt—to save them—so they can go to heaven. But what did the Book of Exodus teach us concerning their deliverance? It taught us that the people were delivered by the sacrifice of the Passover lamb. That is the only way you can be delivered too, not by obeying Mr. Law in the school of life. The Law was given to a delivered people and was *not* the means of escape from Egypt. Faith in applying the blood of the lamb was the only way to escape the judgment of God . . . and don't let us forget it!

Then why the Law? It was given for living in Canaan. This was how the delivered people were expected to live. They were about to enter the Promised Land and needed some rules for living in it. They also needed a God-given culture to make them distinct. The rules they were given required obedience. We know that generation wandered around for 40 years and the people weren't obedient to the Law they were given. But because you are not obedient doesn't mean that God's Law is obsolete, or that God's grace ceases. Knowing that His people would not graduate, He still instructed them and gave them promises.

There were basically two parts to the Law. First, the Commandments of the Decalogue which you find in Exodus 20, and second, the ceremonial law or the ordinances that had to do with worship. I used to think that the Law was the Ten Commandments. The Law *is* the Ten Commandments, plus the ceremonial ordinances. You can read all of these in Exodus 21 through the Books of Leviticus and Numbers.

A High Standard

What was the point of it all? The Decalogue, which we're considering at the moment, taught two things: the awesome holiness of God and the exceeding sinfulness of man. The ceremonial ordinances taught sinful man how to approach an outraged God, and how he would be forgiven and have communion with Him. The schoolmaster's first lesson to his pupils was that it is a frightening, terrible thing to fall into the hands of a holy God. God revealed His own holiness in His laws. A good God could not give bad laws. The Ten Commandments are good laws, and so you know that only somebody who was good and holy could think up these rules. They contained the highest standards, from the highest One. How else could it be?

Against that holy standard, the exceeding sinfulness of man showed up. The Law was given to show man that he had not measured up. Paul wrote that "the law is a schoolmaster to bring us to Christ" (Gal. 3:24). So if anybody asks you the reason for the Law, that's it, in a nutshell. The Law is the schoolmaster to bring you to Christ, who was the only One who ever succeeded in keeping it all, and who can enable you to live it. The Law was not given to deliver us from the judgment of God because we think we've kept it. That's what the majority of people believe in many churches today, and they're wrong. Dreadfully, terribly, terrifyingly wrong, because they are not going to go to heaven if they keep the Ten Commandments. Do you know why? If only people who have kept the Ten Commandments go to heaven, it's going to be empty! Man has never perfectly kept the Ten Commandments, yet people go on trying to do the best they can and hope it's good enough. But it isn't!

The Law was given to show us we've come short of God's standard. It is a measuring stick, and it shows the exceeding sinfulness of man. Paul wrote, "All have sinned and come short [of the standard] of the glory of God" (Rom. 3:23). "All" means you and me. There is no exception, in case you thought you were it! Every single person on God's earth has come short of the standard. Even if you started today and kept every single one of the Ten Commandments, what about all the ones you've broken before you arrived at this state of perfection? You see, you haven't done it.

We've All Come Short

If you aren't convinced you've got an "F" from the schoolmaster, let's have a quick look at these Commandments. I often meet people who say, "I live by the Sermon on the Mount, and I don't need that Christianity stuff." I have never heard anything so stupid in my life, because the Sermon on the Mount amplifies the Ten Commandments and makes them harder still to keep.

When we begin to talk to people who say, "I live by the Ten Commandments, but I can do it without God," we are talking with people who are breaking the first and greatest Commandments of all. That God is supreme is what the first commandment is all about. God says it's a big sin to ignore Him and think you can make it on your own. Let's look at the next commandment, "Thou shalt have no other gods before Me." He was talking about idols that represent a spirit. "You shall not worship spirits," He said, yet today there are 30,000 witches' covens in Britain alone, and there are more than that in the U.S.A. and Canada. And so this word is very relevant. There are people in our age rushing all over the place to worship spirits, and today they are not even bothering with the idols that represent them! They are ignoring God's revelation of Himself.

The sacredness of God's name must not be violated. Some of us who work in offices, or go to high school, know that blaspheming God's holy name seems to be the normal thing to do, yet God says, "I will not hold him guiltless that takes My name in vain." I think we need to be careful. There are also derivations of God's name that Christians use all the time. Jesus said, "Let your yea be yea; and your nay . . . nay" (James 5:12).

Is the schoolmaster showing you that you have come short? The Law talks about the sanctity of the Sabbath. "If thou turn away thy foot from the Sabbath, from doing thy pleasure on My holy day; and call the Sabbath a delight, the holy of the Lord, honorable, and shalt honor Him, not doing thine own ways nor finding thine own pleasure, nor speaking thine own words; then shalt thou delight thyself in the Lord" (Isa. 58:13-14). What do you do with your Sabbath? Do you follow your own pleasure instead of trying to please Him on

His holy day? Well then, you've broken the Sabbath, according to the Scriptures. The Sabbath is for rest and for spiritual enrichment and exercise.

What about the sanctity of the family, which is dealt with in the Ten Commandments? The honor due to parents, and the parents' responsibility for the children's behavior? God holds the parents responsible for the children's attitude to Him. That's a heavy thing. We are to bring our children up in the nurture and admonition of the Lord.

The sanctity of human life is guarded by the commandment, "Thou shalt not kill." Is this abused? In 1973, one million abortions, or baby murders, were legally executed. How many more illegally? People are killing themselves with alchohol or drugs all over our nation today, and the sanctity of human life is under fire. "Thou shalt not kill yourself, or anybody else," God says.

The schoolmaster says that life has value, but in our day and age the media does not consider that to be news, or it doesn't make for good ratings. Today, people are not learning the teacher's lessons: the sanctity of God's name, the sanctity of the Sabbath, the sanctity of the family, the sanctity of human life, the sanctity of marriage; all these are courses in human behavior that people willfully refuse to take or major in.

When Jesus came, He explained the schoolmaster's teachings. "Thou shalt not commit adultery" was amplified in Matthew 5:28. "Thou shalt not have one lustful thought," He said, "because that is how adultery happens." Have you and I ever had one lustful thought? Then we have broken the Ten Commandments. And the Bible says that if you have ever broken one, you are guilty of breaking them all (James 2:10). Mr. Law is the schoolmaster, and Mr. Law is a perfectionist; even if we get 99 on our exam paper, we need to know that the pass mark is 100.

The sanctity of personal property, summed up in the words, "Thou shalt not steal," and the sanctity of our neighbor's reputation, guarded by the words, "Thou shalt not lie," were laid on us at that ancient mountain site. "You must not be envious of your neighbor's house, or want to sleep with his wife, or want to own his slaves, oxen, donkeys, or anything else he has" (Ex. 20:17, LB). In other words, we must not covet.

And so, if anybody comes to me and says, "Hey, I live by the Ten Commandments" I say, "Well, I'm very glad to meet you, you're the first person, apart from Jesus Christ, that ever has, and I think you're terrific." The Law was given for a purpose, and it still has that purpose for us today. The Law is a schoolmaster to bring us to Christ, who alone has fulfilled the Law, and can come within us and enable us to begin to obey it too.

Mr. Law teaches that you have failed His class, you have got an "F" on your report card! The punishment of an "F" is His disapproval and condemnation (see John 3:18).

But don't forget, there was another part of the Law given by God to Moses. That was the part called the ordinances. This ceremonial law was for those who acknowledged they had made an "F." Sinful man could bring a required offering and be forgiven. The offering was the perfect lamb, that bore the curse and the punishment for him, as demanded by the Law. It was the man's substitute for judgment.

In Galatians 3:23-25, we read, "Before faith came, we were kept under the Law, shut up unto the faith which should afterwards be revealed. Wherefore the Law was our school-master to bring us to Christ, that we might be justified by faith. But after that faith is come, we are no longer under a schoolmaster." True, we are no longer under the school-master when we have left school, but we are expected to live out the lessons he taught us.

The Law will lead you to the living Lamb, who is Christ, so don't decide you can grow up and have no need of school. You are not beyond keeping God's rules as you live in Canaan. The schoolmaster will instruct you how to know Christ, who will impart to you the power to live the promised life in the Promised Land.

Worksheet for Group Study

If Christ gives us power to keep His Law we need not then wonder how we should live in Canaan; we already have been instructed. Study the Ten Commandments, and remember, we are not under the Law but under Grace. Grace is the means by which the power is made available for us to be law-abiding citizens of heaven while we are still on earth. Oh yes, on earth!

The Ten Commandments

1. Read Exodus 20, Exodus 31:18, and Deuteronomy 5:22.

    a. How was the Law given? (See Ex. 20:1.)

    b. Who was it given to? (See Ex. 31:18.)

2. "Thou shalt have no other gods before Me." Look up these related verses:

Deuteronomy 6:5; 2 Kings 17:35; Jeremiah 24:7

How does God describe Himself in Exodus 20:5-6?

Read Isaiah 43:1; because of this fact, in all things He shall have the preeminence (see Col. 1:18; Phil. 2:10-11).

3. What does God say the effects and results of spirit worship will be? (See Ex. 32:33; Lev. 19:31; 20:6; Isa. 44:10-11; Ex. 20:5, 20; Jer. 25:8-11; Deut. 5:9.) Apply the verses to a modern situation.

4. "Thou shalt not take the name of the Lord thy God in vain." (See Ex. 20:7; Lev. 19:12; Matt. 5:33-37; Matt. 15:18-19; Col. 3:8.) Discuss how we should react in an office or school situation to others casually or heatedly blaspheming God's name.

5. Read Exodus 20:8 and write a paragraph about your Sabbath. Be honest; is it a joy or a bore? Why? What is forbidden in Scripture? (See Isa. 58:13-14.) What is commanded? (See Ex. 20:8-11; Ex. 23:12; Ex. 31:13-16; Lev. 23:3; Mark 3:4; Col. 2:16; Luke 13:15-16.)

6. What should you do if your father or mother tells you to do something wrong? Is it right to honor them and obey? (See Matt. 15:4; Eph. 6:1-4; Col. 3:20.) Or should you

obey God rather than man? (See Col. 3:25; Acts 5:29; Acts 4:19; Matt. 12:50.)

7. Look up Matt. 5:21; Mark 10:19; Luke 18:20. What is the root of the fruit of murder? What is the antidote for anger? (See 1 John 3:11; 1 John 3:15-16; Ps. 37:1-8; Ecc. 7:9; Eph. 4:26, 31-32.)

8. What should my Canaan marriage be like? What does God think of adultery? (See Lev. 20:10; Eph. 5:22-33; Heb. 13:4; Mark 10:8-9.)

9. Look up Matthew 19:18; Mark 10:19; Romans 13:9. Is there anything you should make restitution for, now that you live in Canaan? (Ex. 22:1, 3, 9)

10. Write out Leviticus 19:19 and memorize it—now. Look up Romans 12:19 as well.

11. Compare Romans 7:7 and 13:9. What is the antidote for covetousness? (See Rom. 10:10; Luke 12:15.)

To summarize this study, write a paragraph on what a new believer's attitude should be to the Law.

9

The Sacred Cow

Not only was Amalek in Canaan, but the devil was there, too. He must have swum across the Red Sea! He obviously had not drowned along with the Egyptians. He was there, and waiting. He intended to challenge Israel every step of the way into the Promised Land. Young Christian, learn this lesson: he who stood behind Pharaoh in Egypt seeking to keep you in bondage will meet you in Canaan. Having retired to lick his wounds over your redemption experience, he will regroup and attack.

Essentially, he has one major goal. His aim in life was, and is, to stop the Word of God getting to the people. With this in mind, he busied himself planting seeds of discontent in the minds of the Children of Israel concerning Moses, God's mouthpiece. He worked on drawing their attention to their physical discomforts, knowing that if they muttered long enough, they would not be able to hear God's explanations. He surely instigated Amalek to attempt to overcome the Israelites.

Suddenly, however, he faced a new problem. So far, God's Law had been given orally. Now, two huge stones were being prepared and engraved supernaturally with words which would be his death knell if obeyed. While Moses was on the mountain receiving those solid blocks of stone, the devil went to work, moving quickly before Moses reappeared with that indelible Rule Book. It is important to note his methods and learn how he operates (see Ex. 32).

Why the Delay?

The writer of the Book of Exodus states (32:1) that the devil used delay. His devices have not changed. As young Christians, we tend to want everything right away, and he knows that sign of immaturity. Which of us who have small children do not know the stamping of a toddler's foot, whose immediate demands are not met. They will not wait. Maybe you need to have a clear word from God concerning the way you should go. Like Israel, you camp at the foot of the mountain and wait for instruction from above. Should you take that job? Should you join that church? Should you date that boy? You wait, but Moses, or whoever is God's human spokesman, is conspicuous by his absence. So in your immaturity, you allow the devil to stop the Word of God getting to you. You will not wait! But you must learn that delay is part of maturity. In the waiting, you are supposed to be growing up. Always remember, God has prepared a Word for you on the mount. He has also prepared a right moment to deliver it. He will not leave you uninstructed. If you are not sure, wait until you are sure. You do not need to ask, "Why the delay?" as a small child would ask. Grow up! God is in no hurry; He is testing you, wanting to know if you are willing to wait for your instructions, instead of running ahead of Him.

If ever I am unsure of a way to act, or if I have a big decision to make, and am not clear as to God's Word about it, I begin to read the word He prepared for me—the Bible. I try to promise God I will wait until I read some principle, or until I see some parallel to my situation in Scripture. Until I am sure I have His commandment, I dare not move away from the foot of the mount. In my experience of life, there have been delays. Sometimes it is because I have not known where to read for my help. Other times, He has had His own good unrevealed reasons for it. I have tried not to let the devil use delay to push me into impatient disobedience. That is what he desires to do, for this way, he will prevent the Word of God getting to the people.

Disillusionment

Another tactic the devil will use is *disillusionment*. It may be disillusionment with the leader, as it was in our text. "As for this Moses," the Children of Israel scathingly said, "we know not what is become of him." (See Ex. 32:1.) "He used to lead us, now he's off to a holy huddle up his religious mountain, and he's left us behind." Maybe if your Moses, who led you out of Egypt, seemed to lose interest in you and you were hurt, you know what I'm talking about. Or perhaps the life God promised you just didn't seem to be materializing, and in your heart you turned back to Egypt. This latter is exactly what the Bible says made these people sin. Read about it in the new Testament, in Acts 7:39.

Turning back in their hearts meant, as far as they were concerned, deciding that other religions had something to offer them after all. So they asked for gods like the Egyptians. They did not reject the idea that they needed gods to go before them (v. 1). They simply began to adhere to those other religious beliefs that had been part and parcel of their environment until now. Those beliefs suddenly seemed as good as their own.

It is dreadfully possible to be a redeemed Christian and be turned aside by the sacred cows of man's speculative philosophies and religions. How many teenage enthusiastic new believers today have found Christ and fallen prey almost at once to the Rev. Moon's religion, or to the Children of God? They looked to the established church to accept them, but in the delay of those older believers' struggles with the youths' appearance or life-styles, they fell prey to some modern sacred cow. The New Testament bears witness to this. Many wolves in sheep's clothing will be waiting for the appearance of new lambs on the scene. The devil will be waiting for delay or disillusionment, and will have a sacred cow in mind to take God's place. In this way, he will have achieved his desired result. He will have stopped the Word of God from building the people up and establishing them in the faith.

Delight's Illusion

The next way the devil will try to achieve his ends may be *delight*. All this waiting for a law that demands such effort! Is it really worth it? "No," says the devil, "you shouldn't get so serious." If it's going to be a lot of "Thou shalt nots" it's not the sort of religion you should have got involved with in the first place. What you probably haven't learned as a new Christian is that the devil has his own "Thou shalt nots." Do you remember that he said to Eve, "Ye shall not surely die"? (Gen. 3:4) The difference between the devil's "Thou shalt nots" and God's, is that his are lies and God's are truth. His lies bring death and suffering, while God's truth brings life and happiness.

The devil said to the Children of Israel, "Enjoy yourselves, you are made to have fun." The people listened to him and "sat down to eat and to drink, and rose up to play" (Ex. 32:6). "Thou shalt not be so serious-minded," Satan had said. "Thou shalt enjoy thyself." God wants us to enjoy ourselves, but knows there is a time and place for it (Ecc. 3:1-8). This was not the time and place for a party, but the devil used delight to distract them from waiting on God. He told them a terrible lie. He said that play was more important than prayer, while hiding the fact that playing with God's rules leads to plagues (v. 35). You cannot play the fool with God and get away with it. God's "Thou shalt nots" protect our joy. The devil's lies lead to the destruction of our very lives. Exodus 33:4 states that the people *mourned* and stripped themselves of their ornaments. The very articles they had given Aaron to worship (32:2) they flung away as they realized the devil's lie; they should have waited on God as He told them too. He will use the illusion of delight, fun, or play to prevent the Word of God getting to the people.

Depravity

The devil also will use *depravity*. Look at v. 25: The people were naked. How far away can you get from God's laws of purity and modesty? Even their enemies would hear of it and be disgusted. Young Christian, it's possible to live in Canaan and sink as low as this. You can find redeemed men and women leaping around at parties without their clothes on, while even their enemies reject that sort of behavior. It's true and is happening today; it's one way the devil will stop the Word of God getting to the people. Which people? The enemies who are watching, and whom God wants to convert into His friends. Note that it was Aaron who led them into this abuse. Aaron, the high and holy spiritual leader!

Despondency

Lastly, the devil will use *despair*. Moses literally had God's Rule Book in his very own hands to present to the people, and he threw his golden opportunity away. In that awful situation, when he saw what the Children of Israel were doing, he allowed Amalek to triumph over him. His old anger burned as the devil furiously fanned the flame, and casting the tables of stone out of his hands, *he* broke the Law! Satan achieved his desired end. He had prevented the Word of God from getting to the people.

How many ministers leave the ministry each year? How many missionaries return home? How many Christian deacons and elders resign from office, casting away the Word of God entrusted to them? They do not throw it away because they cannot believe it, or because they do not live by it, but because, like Moses, they are overcome with despair. If they leave their murmuring, muttering congregation alone for even a short space of time, what happens? Disobedience, disillusionment, and depravity.

If the devil can, he will. Will what? Anyhow, anyway, anytime, stop the Word of God getting to the people! He'll attack the listeners, and he'll attack the messengers of the Truth that sets man free.

Two Were Determined

But there is one fantastic thing about this narrative. It is a word also beginning with "D," but it is to do with God. It is the word *determination*. The devil is busy, but God is committed to speak and to work with those who will listen. Though man may ignore, disobey, or break His Word, it does not alter the truth or the worth of it. It doesn't dissipate the power of it. The written Word, the living Word abides forever. God used a Word to tell Abraham, Isaac, and Jacob that He would bring them into the Promised Land (see 33:1), and because He stands behind His promises, He would not let the devil, or His own chosen people, frustrate His purposes.

God would find some who believed. He would bring in those who, like Caleb, wholly followed Him and, like Joshua, would stake their lives on His assurance. Only two out of a nation were undefeated. The rest perished because of unbelief. But two were sufficient, and the devil could not stop them. Even the unbelief of their parents could not prevent the children from entering in. The Law would be written again on new tablets of stone and pronounced afresh to the people. The schoolmaster would set up school again, and the pupils would have a chance to enroll. No matter how bright the sacred cow had glistened, it would not be allowed to blind the few who would hear, believe, and decide to be on the Lord's side (v. 26).

To be on the Lord's side means you will be dedicated to waiting for the Word, whatever the delay, disillusionment, or depravity you find in your soul, or in other people. To be on the Lord's side means you will be determined to deliver the Word to the people He sends you to.

If you have failed, like Israel or Moses, then repent, climb Horeb one more time, and "hew thee out again the law of God which ye broke" (see Ex. 34:1).

Worksheet for Group Study

1. Recap and discuss the following ways the devil tries to prevent the Word of God getting to the people:

    a. Delay; disillusionment; depravity, despair.

    b. Share any personal illustrations you can think of to illustrate these points.

2. The sacred cow illustrates the glistening lure of other ways of worship and different beliefs. Look up the following verses in the New Testament, and make a list of the ways we can help ourselves recognize an invitation, even by an Aaron, to "set up other gods to go before us."

    a. Read 2 Timothy 3:13-17. What is the warning here? What is the exhortation?

    b. Read 1 John 4:1-4. The "little children" are warned about the false prophets. How can we test their message?

Write out and memorize verses 2 and 3a. Who will help us to overcome them? Where is He?

    c. Read 2 Peter 2:1-3. Describe how these false teachers will work. List the words that describe their methods.

    d. As teachers of God's truth, we are instructed how to act. Not as Moses did—reacting in anger—but according to 2 Timothy 2:24-26.

Even when the people you teach refuse to listen (2 Tim. 4:3-4), you have your orders as a minister of the Gospel (v. 5). Write this verse out in capital letters and memorize it.

It would be a good idea if you are working in a group, or individually, to read some small concise work at this point on cults and other religions.

I recommend Dr. Walter Martin's tapes for study and reference. His address is One Way Library, Division of Vision House Publishers, 1507 East McFadden Avenue, Santa Ana, California 92705.

Or read the *Spirit of Truth and the Spirit of Error* booklet by Keith L. Brooks (Chicago: Moody Press, 1976).

If you spend too much time studying error you can get

more confused. Rather, give priority to study of the truth and you will learn to discern error. I have heard that the employees of some banks are given a period of practice handling and studying real money so that they may learn to spot the counterfeit.

Many attractive sacred cows invite our worship today. Let us learn to recognize and refuse to bow down to them.

10

Restrained from Bringing

Having instructed Israel in the way they should *walk* in the Land of Promise, God began to instruct them in the way they should *worship*. (See Ex. 35—36:7.) Implicit instructions were given to Moses on that holy mountain about the construction of a house for God to dwell in. He promised to come and tabernacle among them, manifesting His visible Presence, so they would be encouraged by the sign of His dwelling. The house that was to be built would not contain all of God, for as the Scriptures say, "the heaven of heavens cannot contain [Him]" (1 Kings 8:27). He doesn't dwell in places made with hands (Acts 7:48; 17:24). Yet He deigned to meet with Israel in Person, in a structure made according to His own calling and design (Heb. 8:5).

Walk and worship must go together. Worship means "attributing worth to a being or person." As we come to know and understand the Person we attribute worth to, we, though crippled with wrongdoing, shall be led to lean on His arm and be enabled to walk in newness of life.

Worship is not merely gazing up at heaven dewy-eyed. Part of worship is work. If to worship God means to spend time acknowledging His worth, then it follows He is worth doing things for. This is also a form of worship. If only pastors could get across to their congregations the fact that worship incorporates work, they would be in the same gloriously embarrassing position of the folks in charge of building the tabernacle. We would need to restrain the people from bringing. What were they giving? Read Exodus 36:1-7.

Practical Worship

Moses had been up the mountain and received a pattern, or blueprint, for the building of this huge church in the wilderness. Having reported to the people, the time had come for a response from them. The response was quite overwhelming. It wasn't a question of squeezing a dollar or two out of reluctant members. God told them what was needed and they matched their possessions and abilities to the needs of the church. That's worship.

So many people today think that worship is singing in the choir or a preaching ministry. They believe it is a passive or active exercise, but definitely a "spiritual" thing. I believe that practical service can be considered to be spiritual worship.

There's a story told of Jesus going back to heaven and being asked by the angels, "To whom did You entrust the message of salvation?" Jesus pointed out big old Peter busy putting his foot in his mouth, James and John having their usual Sons-of-Thunder row, Thomas running around doubting everybody and everything, and Andrew tied up in a knot of inadequacy. "I've left it with them," He said simply. "But Master," they said aghast, "what happens if they fail?" Quietly Jesus replied, "I have no other plans."

That's heavy, unless He left them and us with tools to do the job, and of course He did. "Faithful is He that calleth you, who also will do it" (1 Thes. 5:24). He equipped us with the technical talent, the instruments of our natural abilities, and with the empowering Holy Spirit, who gifted us with spiritual abilities as well.

We must realize that natural talents are not necessarily spiritual gifts. Many unbelievers are wonderfully talented people. But no unbeliever is spiritually gifted. You can't be spiritually gifted without the Holy Spirit. Can spiritual gifts be practical? Yes, but before I confuse you, let us simply look at our text and endeavor to confine ourselves to what we can learn from this passage about the tools we can use to worship God.

We can all agree that an offering is a religious, spiritual sort of thing. Right? The work-worship God asked for from His people at this point was a work-offering. Let's look at *how* the offering was to be offered. The how of worship was very simple. They were to offer whatever they brought with a willing heart. The people were told it was to be a voluntary, not a compulsory, thing (35:5, 29). God has much to say on this point. Paul told us not to give grudgingly or of necessity, but hilariously, for God loves the hilarious giver (see 2 Cor. 9:7).

What parent doesn't understand this? How often do you ask your youngsters for some service, and decide to do without when met with a grudging sullen face? Oh, what a joy to receive a cheerful, "Sure, Mom." A willing heart is worth all the world, isn't it? Sitting in a pew, because there's no way out of it, isn't worship. That's an offering God does not ask for and will not accept. Over and over again, God asks for those with willing hearts to worship Him with their work.

Special Talents

Consider also *what* they gave. They gave according to their natural abilities, but notice their natural abilities had been polished and disciplined until they were like fine instruments, ready for the surgeon's hand. Kenneth Taylor paraphrased it this way: "Come, all of you who are skilled craftsmen having special talents, and construct what God has commanded us" (35:10, LB).

God gives each of us talents. They are like raw material hidden in a mountainside; gems buried under fauna. We must dig up those hidden properties we find in the earth of our lives and begin to polish and shape them for display. When they are ready, we can bring them voluntarily to Him as an offering, and ask Him where He wants these gems set. This is exactly what the people did. Those who could weave did so, and brought the finished product; those who could carve wood presented their craftsmanship. Those who had no such talent but had strong arms and healthy bodies, offered to carry and haul the heavy materials into place. Those who had abilities to work precious metals set them apart for the service of the Lord.

Stop a moment and think of your natural talents. What is it you are really better at than anything else? What practical work is very easy for you to do? Have you ever dedicated that to Him and realized that He considers it just as much an offering of worship as some spiritual ability?

When I first came to Christ, I remember someone telling me I needed to dedicate, or set apart, my natural abilities for God's service. If I really thought He was worth it, then He should have the use of those things He had gifted me with in the first place. I made a list. My tennis and ice-skating ability. What ever was He going to do with that? My artistic ability. I did love writing letters to friends, so I put that down. I had no way of knowing at the time that the practice I would have in that direction would lead into writing Christian books. My love of dramatic art. All these were things I was moderately good at before I knew Jesus. Things I had brought out of Egypt with me like the Children of Israel had brought those jewels and materials into the Promised Land.

I gave them to God and told Him that if He could use them, to do so. He did, and He has been ever since. Everyone is a tennis nut in England, and God gave me the idea of staging and running a tennis tournament for my area. I was able to do this because of my own ability. However, instead of playing in it to win, I used to draw together hundreds of people to enjoy a marvelous day of sport, and finish up with a huge open-air barbecue, with music and a spiritual message.

We reached many, many people. Winning souls was far more thrilling than winning tennis tournaments. I've done both so I can testify to that.

I gave God my artistic and dramatic abilities and immediately found use for them in creating a play we used in the streets and coffee bars of Europe, to meet and reach the unreached. I have yet to use my ice-skating, but maybe one of these days we'll do that little art and drama play on ice! Why not? Imagine the audience that would gather for that one. A friend of mine brought her creative art abilities to Jesus and now she teaches six art classes, all involving Bible messages and witnessing. She also has the opportunity to go to society clubs, taking her art with her and drawing spiritual parallels from the different stages of a piece of work.

Worship involves bringing a willing offering of our natural abilities, and when we have worked to polish and discipline them, God will put us and our talents to work. He will also give us certain detailed instructions about where and how to use them. The details given in Exodus 36 were minute. It was absolutely clear where each talent was needed. Can you sew? Sew for Jesus. Can you landscape? Ask Him where, when, and how. What gift did you bring with you from Egypt to Canaan? Will you not worship Him with it?

When do we bring our talents to Him? The answer is everyday! (Ex. 36:3) Every day, until He tells you to stop. Not on Sundays, or once a year at the church bazaar; we must begin to be more creative than that. When your church has got too much of everything and there is no more room for you or your talents, then you can have a rest.

Mathematics, Music, or Crafts?
Some people are talented in many areas. And so occasionally we need to spend a season in prayer and ask God which talents He wants us to polish and use for a particular time, and which He wants us to lay aside. God was more specific in His instructions to Moses to bring exactly those things that were required *at that time* for the building of the tabernacle.

Later, other gifts were needed, such as music and maintenance abilities. When we have dedicated ourselves to God, then it follows He is the One who guided us to certain areas of service at specific times.

At one time in Stuart's life, he used his musical talent in a singing group; then that was laid aside for mathematical talent needed to keep the accounts of a missionary society.

A few years ago, my creative art and craft abilities were tested to the full, putting together a nursery school with very few funds. This school was to be an outreach to the city. It had to pass stringent government requirements to be registered, and as it was to be held in an old and broken-down warehouse, with dead dogs and rats in the basement, lots of practical talent was needed! I begged ends of wooden planks from lumber yards, and cut, polished, and painted pictures on them for building blocks. We made paints from powders and dyes. Creating water troughs and sand trays was easy, but the musical instruments were more difficult. It's amazing, though, how you can create a whole band from metal coat hangers, empty bottles, tin cans, and beans!

Our nursery school was not only passed by the authorities, but became *the* place to send your children. I well remember talking a brewer into letting me have barrels which we cut in half for tables, and making climbing apparatus from the local tire junkyard. I loved every minute of that three month endeavor, and God used my practical talents to begin a venture that now serves over 250 children and pays the salaries of three missionaries. Since then, He has not asked me to use those particular talents, but they are stored away ready to be used again if and when He chooses.

The willingness to be directed by Him is what is important. To take up or lay down whichever tool He asks for, when He asks for it.

It's interesting to see what the Bible says about the man God called to supervise and teach others these practical crafts for the building of the tabernacle. Exodus 35:31 states that God filled Bezaleel with His Spirit for "all manner of workmanship." When we recognize that our practical abilities are gifts from God, and dedicate them willingly to Him, He will fill us with His Spirit, who will impart to us the know-how to worship Him with our skills. So a Spirit-filled person is not just a person who prays, preaches, or witnesses for Christ, but one whose workmanship is the vehicle for God's power and manifestation.

Spiritual Abilities

The Bible also teaches that along with our practical talents, the Holy Spirit gifts us with spiritual abilities. These are imparted to us and may or may not be meshed along the same talent lines we have been talking about.

For instance, a teacher may be very effective teaching children in a secular school situation, but may not have a spiritual gift for teaching the Bible. On the other hand, someone never trained technically may discover he has a real gift as a teacher of the Scriptures. Then again, someone trained as a teacher may find himself with a touch of God on his Bible teaching, and realize his spiritual gift runs along the line of his trained natural talent.

The spiritual gifts God gives are for encouraging and building up the body of believers spiritually. They are used for enlisting, enabling, enriching, and encouraging others. The Apostle Paul wrote of special gifts for church office, for church ministry, and for outreach to those outside the body of Christ (1 Cor. 12:1-11).

Stuart has compiled a list of definitions of the special gifts for Christian ministry that may help you to identify the gift God has given to you to exercise. Keep in mind as you read the list that gifts require careful identification.

1. Specific gifts for church office (1 Cor. 12:28; Rom. 12; Eph. 4):

    a. Apostles—purifiers of doctrine, pioneers
    b. Prophets—forthtellers, foretellers of truth
    c. Teachers—instructors
    d. Evangelists—travelling presenters of evangel

     e. Pastors—overseers of congregations

     f. Rulers—those who "stand before"

  2. Special gifts for Christian ministry:

     a. Word of wisdom—ability to explain "wisdom of God"

     b. Word of knowledge—ability to know what you didn't know you knew

     c. Faith—ability to believe God when others are floundering

     d. Healing—ability to convey God's sovereign healing ability

     e. Miracles—ability to be involved with God in doing the unusual

     f. Prophecy—see 1b

     g. Discerner of spirits—ability to evaluate spiritual profession and ministry

     h. Tongues—ability to speak in unknown languages

     i. Interpretation—ability to interpret 2h

     j. Exhortation—ability to encourage

     k. Helpers—ability to be supportive

     l. Acts of mercy—ability to serve and be cheerful about it

Our spiritual gifts need finding, using, and training in the same way as our practical talents. And we need to be careful not to get more enamored with the gifts than with the Giver of those gifts.

Gifts and the Giver

When Stuart used to travel extensively, he would come home to a very excited wife and three equally excited children. Once our children ran to him asking, "What did you bring us, Daddy?" A childish question that was easy to understand and forgive. However, if I had met my husband with the same question, "Dad" would probably have been justifiably hurt. We need to be adult enough to want the Giver of gifts more than those things He brings us. The Corinthian church had become supremely Gift-conscious, to the exclusion of God-consciousness.

It must be remembered, too, that the gifts of the Spirit are not as important as the fruit. As Paul wrote in 1 Corinthians 13, we may speak with the tongues of men or angels, but if our gifts are not exercised in love, we profit nothing. A missionary may be marvelously talented and richly gifted spiritually, but have no self-control. This can lead to total disaster in his relationships with the very people he has traveled thousands of miles and spent many years training to reach.

As far as I can see from Exodus 36, the key to it all is a heart presented to God, in whose hands it is filled with wisdom and stirred to work for Him (v. 2).

When the heart is willingly given, then the rest will follow and the leaders of our churches will hear the glad news Moses heard: "The people bring much more than enough for the service of the work, which the Lord commanded to make. So the people were *restrained* from *bringing*. For the stuff they had was sufficient for all the work to make it, and *too much*" (Ex. 36:5-7).

Let me ask you a question. Would you say this is a description of your Christian work? Is the stuff you are practically producing too much? Is someone going to have to restrain you from bringing? Or are you dwelling in your paneled houses while His house lies waste? (See Haggai 1:4.)

Worksheet for Group Study

Part I
   1. Talents for the Congregation
Read 2 Corinthians 9:7 and Exodus 35:10. What were the two things God was looking for? How does this give you a clue as to your responsibility concerning your talents and how to use them?

If talents are natural abilities given by God, take a minute and think of yours. What are you good at naturally? What do you get A's for? What do you enjoy doing outside school, home, or work for which you have a certain ability? If you are completing this worksheet with a group, go round the group and tell the one natural talent (not spiritual gift) that you think is your best. If you are having trouble, let your friends help you out. If you are on your own, make a list and discuss it with your pastor.

Read Exodus 35:20-29. Where did the people find the gifts they brought? Would it have required time or cost them effort to give them? Why? Who were the two men God called to head the work? (vv. 30 and 34)

Make a list from verses 31 to 35 of 14 things the Spirit of God did with their talents. Chapter 36:1 states that the Eternal gave the know-how for these practical abilities. Do you see how practical talents can be an acceptable offering to God's work in the church?

2. Talents for the World
Read Matthew 25:31-36. Where else must our practical talents be used? Share in the group what practical skills are needed for outreach to the lost (see vv. 35-36).

If you are a teenager, ask yourself how you can be preparing to be useful in your adult life. If you are an adult, discuss how you can begin to practice your skills.

Part II
Though the talents mentioned in Matthew 25:20 are money, the same principle applies.
1. Read the story through to yourself.
2. If you are completing this worksheet as a group, three of you should take the parts of the man with five talents, the man with two talents, and the man with one talent, and tell your stories to the group. Another of you make a list of the rewards of the profitable servants (see vv. 21, 23) and the punishment of the unprofitable servant (see vv. 25-30). Tell the group about them.
3. Look up the following verses on being faithful with our God-given talents, and report what you learn to the group. Or

work on your own with pencil and notebook, and find answers to this question: *What can I discover about being faithful to God with my talents?* Keep in mind that to be faithful means to be trusted.

    a. Who is our Great Example? (Heb. 3:1-2)

    b. Where was Moses faithful? (Num. 13:7)

    c. The writer of Proverbs 25:13 tells us another place we must be faithful. Where is it?

    d. God has a promise for the faithful here. What is it? (See Proverbs 28:20.)

    e. How many things do we need to start and practice, being faithful? (See Matt. 25:21.) Where do we start?

    f. Read Daniel 6:1-5. In what practical areas was Daniel faithful?

    g. What does Luke 16:10 mean? How can we apply this to ourselves?

Part III

1. Read 1 Corinthians 12.

    a. What illustration does the Apostle Paul use to illustrate the different gifts? (v. 12)

    b. Write down 12 things you can learn about gifts from verses 4-27.

2. Read 1 Corinthians 13:1-3. Are the fruit of the Spirit or the gifts of the Spirit most important? Why? The fruit of the Spirit is found in Galatians 5:22-23. Look this up and discuss why these would be more important in a missionary's life than gifts.

3. Think about or discuss the list of gifts of ministry. Do you recognize your own?

Recommended books and tapes:

6-cassette album, *Spiritual Gifts,* by D. Stuart Briscoe

Body Life, by Ray Stedman (Glendale, California: Regal Books, 1972)

The Holy Spirit and His Gifts, by J .Oswald Sanders (Grand Rapids: Zondervan)

Spiritual Gifts and the Church, by Donald Bridge and David
  Phypers (Downers Grove, Illinois: InterVarsity Press)
19 Gifts of the Spirit, by Leslie B. Flynn (Wheaton, Illinois:
  Victor Books, 1974)
Discover Your Spiritual Gift and Use It, by Rick Yohn
  (Wheaton, Illinois: Tyndale House Publishers)

11

The Tabernacle

Many books have been written about the tabernacle. I have loved each lecture given, and illustration used. So it is hard to approach the many chapters that have been so well ploughed over, and seek to drive yet another furrow.

I want us to think about the three parts of the tabernacle and learn what we can about different phases of Christian worship. In my observation, Christians can fall into three categories. Those who enter the outer court of a worship walk with God and stay there; those who, like the priests, continue on into the Holy place; and those who somehow live a lot in the Holiest of All, as Andrew Murray so beautifully calls that most intimate of places. The Holiest of All was the abode of the very presence of God, where He continuously manifested Himself. As New Testament Christians, our position is clear. Unlike our brethren in the wilderness, a way has been made by Jesus to enable us to freely walk wherever we will in our tabernacle experience with God.

I believe it is God's intention that every believer live out his life in the Holiest of All, as well as benefiting from worship in every part of the tabernacle.

I also believe there is no packaged time allowance as to how quickly we may move from one place to another. Each person's growth is different. But I believe with all my heart the way has been made into the Holiest by our Lord Jesus, and you and I may enter into all that has been made available to us. So let us look at this marvelous visual aid built by the Father for His children in the sands of their wanderings.

The tabernacle was to be set up in the very center of the camp. The tribes were told to position themselves around it, each in their given place. The structure where God would live among them had to be in the midst. So it must be with us: God central, with all we have and are, gathered around Him. He is not to be moved off to the circumference, but must take pride of place in our national, social, and personal lives.

The first time the tabernacle was erected, it was easy for the people to do it all just right (Ex. 40). What excitement, what a thrill! What a new and unique experience. But then the journey began. Every time there was a move by that huge congregation, everything had to be packed up in a prescribed way and carried to the next resting place. Sometimes they only stayed a few days in one spot. How tempting not to bother setting it up at all. Or how easy to throw the thing together at the outer ring of the camp and just fellowship together instead.

A decision was needed by the people every single time they moved to set Him in the midst. In case of attack by their enemies, the sacred things could be guarded. We do not watch carefully enough the holy things God has entrusted to us. So often we are guilty of carelessly leaving the things concerning our God scattered in all directions around the outskirts of our camp.

Young Christian, God tells you He wishes to abide in the midst. Only then can He begin to make real His blessings to your heart.

When Jesus rose again from the dead, He walked through a door that was not able to shut Him out and stood in the midst of the disciples. We can try to lock our doors if we like, but He has every glorious intention of walking right through them into His rightful place and commanding our attention (John 14:27).

The Brazen Altar

Many marvelous parallels can be drawn from the tabernacle. The Book of Hebrews explains a lot of it for us. The whole structure reminds and instructs us so much about the Person of the Lord Jesus Christ, our great High Priest who lives within to minister to us, that it pays to take a closer look at some of the details. As soon as we decide to allow God to be in the center of our lives, and we have come through the narrow gate which is the only way into life (Matt. 7:14), we enter into our first worship experience with God. As soon as we begin to worship, we, like our friends in the wilderness, are confronted with the brazen altar, upon which the continually burning sacrifice glows. We, like they, will need to be reminded that a Lamb has been slain and a life given. That brazen altar was a continual reminder to those pilgrims, and I too need some symbols to remind me of Christ's sacrifice.

That is why the Lord's Supper is so important. The broken bread and poured out wine remind us that without the shedding of blood, there is no remission of sin (Heb. 9:22).

Christians need to come to the Lord's Table regularly, just as the people in Exodus days needed to gaze at the brazen altar regularly. They would bring their lamb and impute to it their sin by laying their hands upon its head, and then it would be killed. It was their "at-one-ment" with God. When we come to the Lord's table, we know He has already appeared, once for all, to put away sin by the sacrifice of Himself (Heb. 7:27). We can look back to the day when we, by faith, placed our hands on Him and imputed our sin to our Substitute. "This do in remembrance of Me," He said, and in remembering Him, we are reminded of the price of our redemption and what has been accomplished for us.

The Laver of Cleansing

Next, the people in Exodus days came to the laver of cleansing. This was the bath where a ceremony of foot-washing took place. In the outer court of our first worship experiences with God, we have to learn that our feet need to be continually cleansed. How dirty we get walking around this world, and daily we need Him to take our feet, just as He did in the Upper Room, and wash us clean. For if He does not cleanse us, we cannot go on into the Holy Place.

Let us talk about this for a moment. When you are born anew, He forgives your sin. That is past, present, and future sin. He doesn't just forgive you up to now, for God is outside of now. He made "now" and hung it in a bubble called time. God is all around that bubble as well as in it! So the moment He sees you kneel and ask forgiveness, and sees you accept Jesus as your Substitute, He forgives you everything in the bubble, everything from this moment on, until the day you burst out of it into the "here" with God.

You may ask, "Why, then, do I need to ask forgiveness once I have found Christ—if all my sin is forgiven at that moment of commitment?" The reason is explained by the laver of cleansing. Fellowship with the Father requires shoes off and clean feet! Your relationship depends on your birth, but your fellowship depends on your behavior.

For example, we have a son. In fact, we have two. What would happen if one born in our family chose to be a prodigal, left home, and ran far away to a pigsty of his choice. Well, he would always be our son, for our life would be in him; he has been born into our family. His relationship would never change, for it would depend on his birth. But his fellowship with us would depend upon his behavior. When you've tramped around in a pigsty, and you come to yourself one day and decide to go home and talk to your Father again, then your feet will need cleansing before you can run comfortably around His house. You see, your relationship depends on your birth, but your fellowship upon your behavior, and daily you and I trample in some dirt somewhere, and need Jesus to wash our feet. Not our head and our hands, for we are cleansed from the sin principle in our lives by the Word He has spoken unto us; but from sins that need to be repented of daily because they have ruined our family fellowship with our heavenly Father.

Many Christians stop in the outer court of worship. They know what it is to have been to the brazen altar and they know what it is to say "sorry" prayers and let Jesus keep cleaning them up, but that is all. In fact, the sad thing is that they don't want anything more, or some don't know there *is* anything more for them to have. They think the inner holy places are just for the priests, or mystics. Their worship experience is a pretty self-centered affair.

The Holy Place

But you see, we live this side of the Cross. The way has been made not only into the Holy Place, but into the Holiest of All for all of us (Heb. 10:19). You and I are priests now, for the Bible talks of the priesthood of all believers (1 Peter 2:9). The chief privilege of a priest is access to God, and Jesus made that gloriously possible.

To stay with an experience of a brazen altar and laver of cleansing is not sufficient as far as the One who has graciously come to tabernacle in your midst is concerned. He wants to draw you deeper into worship. He wants to take you to His very heart. There is more of Him that many of you have not yet discovered, and more of you that can involve itself in a prayer experience.

As noted before, many new Christians believe the Holy Place is for priests, pastors, nuns—special people like that. God set a veil across the entrance to both Holy Places in Exodus days and forbade the people entrance. But now you and I may walk in and enjoy what God has for us.

Three pieces of furniture abide in the Holy Place. Firstly, the candlestick. There was light in the Holy Place; light to see by, light to serve by, and light to worship by. Illumination from God who is light and in whom is no darkness at all (1 John 1:5).

As we are drawn nearer to Him in our worship experience,

He will illuminate that time for us. He will lighten our *way*. He has said that His Word will be a lamp to our feet and a light to our path (Ps. 119:105). Sometimes we need to have light shed on an immediate step. We have arrived at a situation, and we aren't sure which way to handle it. Be reminded that He has promised a light for our feet; He will show us clearly where to step. The Word of God will throw light on the whole situation, and as you read, it will be like a voice behind you saying, "This is the way, walk ye in it" (Isa. 30:21). He also promises light ahead for your path. As you look ahead of you into your immediate future, the way may look pretty black and forboding. He is light, and if you are pressing on into a deeper experience of worship, you will find light ahead as well as light around. Even if God calls you to walk through the darkest valley, the valley of the shadow of death, you will find that where there's a shadow, there's always light! God promises you shall not walk in darkness, but shall have the light of life (John 8:12). So as you decide to go deeper, pressing on to know Him more, you will be met by the Golden Candlestick, and will have light for your way.

Jesus said, "I am the Light of the world," and then He said, "*Ye* are the light of the world." We are to be like that Golden Candlestick—bearing high the light. Light for a *world* that is in darkness. That is how we are to function. The candlestick lit up its entire area, and God intends us not to hide our light, but to let it shine.

God promises not only light for our way and light for our world, but light for our *worship*. How can we really worthship God? How can we learn how to praise Him aright? Do we just go on saying, "Thank You, Jesus" all our lives? Is this praise? No, not *only* this. God will throw light on this problem. He will illuminate His Word, and will throw light on difficult passages of Scripture. He will enlighten the eyes of our hearts (Eph. 1:18), to know what a fantastic thing it is to be invited to enjoy an inheritance in Christ. He will enlighten our very worship so we shall begin to see God with our inner eyes. The veil will disappear for the Christian who decides to walk in that Holy Place, and he will begin to see clearly spiritual and heavenly realities.

The presence bread in the Holy Place consisted of twelve loaves, and was sacred food for the priests. Jesus said, "I am the bread of life: He that cometh to Me shall never hunger" (John 6:35). The Christian who insists on pressing toward the Holiest of All will find the presence bread sustaining him for his priestly duties.

God prepared special bread for His priests, and His choicest fare awaits you in the Holy Place. As you grow in knowledge of Him, you will find that God will give you fresh bread daily that you may be strong and vigorous as you serve. When I first began speaking to groups of people, I felt a great dread that I would run out of energy, or food for thought. I have found that as I feasted on Him, the Presence Bread of life, I was strengthened by His might in the "inner man," and God always enabled me to serve those He sent me to. He told me I would fly, but when I couldn't fly anymore I would run; when I couldn't run anymore I would walk, and He told me I would never faint (Isa. 40:31). Many a time I have arrived to take meetings, and recognized the look on the faces at the airport, "Here comes the teacher, let's kill her!" but it's never happened. The Presence Bread keeps me strong. He sustains and energizes me.

Manna for survival is one thing, bread for the priest is another. Paul wrote that we should grow up to more mature eating habits. He told us to learn how to be a workman that needeth not be ashamed, rightly dividing the word of truth (2 Tim. 2:15). We are told to grow from collecting enough manna to keep us alive, and learn to feast as priests of the most High God on the presence bread of Christ Himself. Many books, tapes, and helps are available to take us deeper in that Holy Place. To gather enough for yourself is one thing, but to serve as a priest, you need to gather and feed others too. That sort of appetite is stimulated as you choose to serve in the Holy Place.

The priests presented the prayers of the people at the altar of incense. Maybe it is in this very aspect that you can decipher in which area of worship you are living. In the outer court experience, you have learned to get cleaned up. Your prayer life has been mainly self-centered. "I'm dirty, Jesus," "forgive me, Lord," "clean me up, Saviour." But if you decide to go deeper, you will begin to serve as a priest at the altar of incense. You will present the needs of others before God. You will engage in a ministry of prayer on their behalf. You will begin to know what we were talking about when Moses, Aaron, and Hur prayed for Joshua in the valley.

To live in the light and to be sustained by the bread of the presence is to find the desire to pray at that altar. Do you pray more for yourself than for others? Where are you living in the tabernacle?

The Holy Place is holy. You sense His presence near. You recognize that you are growing, and getting stronger every day. All this is necessary, but friend, even this is not enough. God calls you one step further; He calls you into the Holiest of All.

Across this most sacred of all places, where the manifest presence of God abode, was a heavy veil. Only once a year the great High Priest was allowed to enter in. He carried with him a lamb, perfect and without blemish. A lamb that had been slain. It was the substitute sacrifice for the whole nation. Entering the Holy of Holies, he sprinkled the blood of that animal on the mercy seat, which covered the ark wherein lay the righteous demands of a Holy God, set within the Law.

When Jesus, the Lamb of God, died on the cross, the veil in the temple across the entrance to the Holy of Holies, was rent in two. A way had been made to the mercy seat for you and for me. Then Jesus presented Himself to His holy Father as our substitute, and the Father accepted Him on our behalf. Therefore, *we* may boldly come before the throne of grace because of Him! So little Christian, don't think the Holiest of All is for Aaron the great High Priest of the Book of

Exodus. A way has been made by Jesus, our great High Priest, and He calls you and me to enter into a worship experience, not just to be enjoyed for a few minutes a year on a religious holiday. He calls us to live there, moment by moment, in the most intimate Presence of God. So let us enter in.

Worksheet for Group Study

1. *The tabernacle is the abiding place of God.* In the Old Testament we see the tabernacle as the dwelling place of God—a place where His Shekinah glory marked His presence. In the New Testament, we find that He has a new dwelling place. Note the progression of the dwelling place of God:

a. Moses—tabernacle of God's glory—Exodus 40:34-35; Numbers 14:10; 16:19; 16:42; 20:6.

b. Solomon—temple of God's greatness—1 Kings 8:11; 2 Chronicles 5:14; 7:1.

c. A.D. 33—trophies of God's grace—Acts 7:47-50; 17:24; 1 Corinthians 3:16-17; 6:19-20; 2 Corinthians 6:16.

2. *The tabernacle is the activity place of God.* The conspicuous presence of God in the Old Testament could be found in a building like the tabernacle or temple. In the New Testament, He is conspicuously present and active in our bodies. What activities should take place in our bodies if they are the activity center of God? (See 1 Cor. 6:13, 19-20; 13:3; 12:27; 2 Cor. 4:10; Rom. 6:12; 8:13; Gal. 6:17; Phil. 1:20; James 3:2.)

3. *The tabernacle is the access place of God.* In the Book of Hebrews we see Christ contrasted with the Levitical system of sacrifices—the latter portrayed as a shadow of the real thing. What do these verses tell us about such a contrast and the access we now have to God? Hebrews 8:1-6; 4:14-16; 9:13-14; 10:19-25; 12:28-29; 13:7-17

12

Caleb
and the Cloud

Josiah looked anxiously from his tent toward the center of the camp. He sighed with relief and relaxed, for there it was! Father God had known small boys would find it difficult to get to sleep in the dark in a strange environment, and so He had kindly provided an enormous night-light for His young ones.

Josiah was very small. So many traumatic events had been occupying his heart and mind in recent days that he could hardly remember his home in Egypt. But the memories he did have were fearful and horrible indeed. He couldn't forget the sight of his mother weeping silently as she bathed the taskmaster's torturous whip marks on his father's back; and he knew he would forever remember his aunt's frenzied attempts to prevent the cruel soldiers feeding her newborn baby to the crocodiles in the Nile. Little wonder he needed a night-light to brighten the darkness of those thoughts.

Josiah's mind went back to the first time he had seen Father God switch on that marvelous night-light. It had happened after their escape from Pharaoh. As the angel of death passed over the blood-marked doorposts of the Children of Israel, taking to himself the pride of Egypt's children, Josiah watched his nation run away. His father Caleb had lifted him in his strong arms to a vantage point on his shoulders, where he could see everything that was happening, and young though he was, he realized his people were going to be free.

Never having been free, it was difficult for him to comprehend the meaning of the word. Maybe it meant no more Pharaoh? It was at that moment, looking back, that he saw something that showed him that being free didn't mean that! Pursuing them furiously were Egypt's best men of war. Josiah could still see the enemy, but he looked pale and insignificant, and kind of funny, when you looked at him through the manifest Presence of God.

So being free meant peace in the company of the enemy. God in between—Him and me, he thought. "Is it all right to go to sleep?" he whispered to the warm fiery light. "Yes, little one," answered Father God. "He that keepeth Israel shall neither slumber nor sleep, so there's no point in both of us staying awake!"

With that marvelous commodity called childlike faith, Josiah believed God, smiled happily, and fell asleep across his father's shoulders.

In the morning the first thing he did was look for the fiery pillar. It was gone. He began looking in all directions for a sight of it, and suddenly became aware of people excitedly pointing at a strange shape gliding across the desert at the head of the company. At first Josiah thought the sky had fallen down, but then something about that cloud struck him as endearingly familiar, and he knew without anyone telling him, that that strange phenomenon was his night-light. As long as he gazed at it, that calm sense of well-being enveloped him as it had the previous night, and suddenly he knew he never wanted to lose sight of that cloud again. Somehow he realized life could only be meaningful within the radius of its influence (see Num. 13).

Being a child, Josiah couldn't articulate words like *radius* and *influence,* but I believe at some point in a childlike way, his little heart reached out toward that cloud and said,

"Cloud, I will follow You forever, I will run after You until I can run no more, and I will seek to wholly follow You."

The Glory of the Lord

The younger we are when we learn to overcome by the manifest Presence of God, the better. If we allow Him to overcome us, we will find that He will also overcome all that has been overcoming us! To decide to fully follow Him is the prerequisite to His fully filling us with the necessary enabling. In other words, the Cloud will not fill our earthly tabernacle, as it did that desert structure unless we have been obedient and are ready to follow further instructions. The writer of Numbers 9:15-23 explains that a decision to be obedient is necessary if the Glory of the Lord is to be seen.

It is interesting to see what happened to the tent in this passage of Scripture. It sort of disappeared! As the people gazed at a structure full of God, they saw a dim shape of the earthly tabernacle, but the *glory* filled their vision. The writer states, "so it was always" (v. 16).

When Paul, writing to the Ephesian Christians, commanded them to be "filled with the Spirit" he was saying, "so it can be always." A decision to wholly follow the Lord in obedience will result in a definite sense of the Presence of God about you. People will dimly see your tabernacle, but will catch a glimpse of the Glory of the Lord.

This can be a continual thing. Look at verse 16; it reads, "day and night." By day and by night the Glory of the Lord was continually manifest. But keep in mind that if the people were to enjoy the Glory they had to endure following the cloud.

If you think about it, following that Cloud must not have been an easy thing. Sometimes it could not have been very convenient. Can you imagine being Josiah's mother, getting all the children to sleep after a day's hard trek through the desert, and suddenly seeing that unpredictable Cloud take off again? "Oh no," she must have said, "not now, not again!" It must have been very tempting to just stay put and rest awhile, hoping to catch up later. But as a Christian, the problem is that you might not catch up again if you lose sight of the Glory of the Lord. You may lose your sense of direction and wander aimlessly until you die. Look at verse 22. That cloud was most unpredictable, but one thing we do know, Caleb's family was obedient, and that little boy learned to ask "when?" and not to ask "why?"

When the Glory of the Lord is the motivating factor in the parents' life, the children will have the best chance in the world of entering into the blessings of the Promised Land. God is glorified when the Cloud fills the tent, and when His people wholly obey.

I remember sitting in a bedroom in England on the way to join my husband in South Africa to minister to the people there. Our three children were scattered around the world, and I felt pretty lonely and homesick for them. I began to ask myself whatever I was doing leaving them! Surely they would be affected? I read this passage and realized that they would be affected if I followed the Cloud to South Africa, but they would only be affected for good. Like Caleb's parents, I must insist on the Glory of the Lord being my priority. In my obedience lay the hope of their blessing. And so indeed it turned out to be. Josiah was certainly blessed by his parents' obedience, and so were our three teenagers—that period being a marvelous experience for them of growth in God.

But there came a time when other parents were not obedient. Then God blessed Caleb's family for their commitment. What a testimony God gave to Caleb! (See Num. 14:24.)

Caleb, God's Servant

The first thing God said about Caleb was that he was His *servant*. The joys of personal victory are wrapped up in the joys of personal service. Don't forget that serving God doesn't only mean priestly tabernacle service. It involves your gifts and abilities, in fact, all you are as a person, and it involves serving your fellowman.

Numbers 13:1-3 states that Caleb had become a ruler of his tribe. He was one of the leaders of Israel. This involved self-sacrificing service. He was asked to hazard his life on the spy mission into Canaan, and he gladly set out on behalf of others to investigate the Promised Land. If God privileges us with the responsibilities of leadership, that must inevitably involve self-sacrifice on behalf of our fellowman.

If God were to tell Moses to write down something about you, do you think he would write down, "he is My servant"? What evidence is there of you hazarding your life for your fellowman?

Caleb's Attitude

God said something else about Caleb. Having talked about his servanthood, He goes on to comment on his spirit. His attitude is contrasted with the grumbling, mumbling, disobedient spirit of the other leadership, and is commended by God (Num. 14:22-24).

I believe God loves a daring disciple: a Daniel who will brave the lions' den, a David who will laugh in a giant's face, a Peter who will leap without his boat (even if he rocks it). There is a marvelous passage of the Bible (Josh. 14:6-15) that shows us this vibrant faith-filled spirit of Caleb.

It's not every man who will take on a mountain full of giants at the ripe old age of 85! His obedient spirit had sustained a strong aggressive attitude concerning war (v. 11). Only in the Christian can you expect a servant and a soldier all rolled up in one. We must serve our fellowman and we must fight our giants. Some of us have a mountain full of giants facing us. Unlike Caleb, we may choose some other avenue for our years of retirement.

A committed follower will tackle the highest mountain, infested with the nastiest giants, with a strong spirit of faith in God, who is as big and powerful as His promises. His prayer request will be, "Give me this mountain," not, "make this mountain disappear from sight." Listen to Caleb: "If the Lord be with me, then I shall be able to drive them out!"

Even in the Promised Land, a Christian life that is really working, there will still be mountains and giants, Jerichos and problems galore. Caleb's Cloud covered Caleb's life, and filled full through following, he could say "He is able, therefore I am able." Check the contrast of unbelieving talk in Numbers 13:31, "We are not able!" Faith doesn't only believe God can, faith believes God will. This was the spirit that God commended in Caleb, His servant.

Caleb's Children

The last thing God had to say about Caleb was a word concerning his seed. God promised blessing to his children: they would possess the land. What do I want for my children? What do you want for yours? I want the blessing of God promised to Caleb. I want nothing less than the Glory Cloud experience for them, and that their main concern should be for the Glory of God. I want God to be able to commend them for their servanthood and their spirit. That's what I want, and I can see from this passage that all that will probably be caught, not taught, as they see me doggedly pursuing the Cloud.

Will you go in, not for your own sake only, but for your children's sake as well? Why don't you possess your possessions? Do I hear you say, as the unbelieving elders did, "But the people are strong, the cities are walled, and the giants are ready to gobble us up," or will you say with Caleb, "Let us go up at once, for we are well able to overcome?"

Worksheet for Group Study

1. Read Numbers 13:26-33. Answer these questions:
     a. What sort of spy are you?
     b. Name some of the giants (things that are bigger than you) that you face.

c. What is the end result of being a bad spy? (Num. 14:1)

2. Read Numbers 14:20-38.

a. How many chances did God give the people? (vv. 22, 27)

b. Note God's care for His children (v. 31).

c. Note the blessings of obedience (vv. 36-38).

3. Read Joshua 14:6-15.

Pray about the strength you need for your particular war. Try to pray like Caleb did, "Give me *this* mountain!"